# FRIENDS AND NEIGHBORS

*by* FLORENCE SCHULZ

A Resource Book for Ministering

to

Primary and Junior Boys and Girls

in

Inner-city Areas

Published for the

COOPERATIVE PUBLICATION ASSOCIATION

THE PILGRIM PRESS · BOSTON

The scripture quotations in this publication are (unless otherwise indicated) from the *Revised Standard Version of the Bible*, copyright 1946 and 1952 by the Division of Christian Education, National Council of Churches, and used by permission.

This is one of a series of books produced for interdenominational use by the Protestant denominations working through the Cooperative Publication Association.

## THE COOPERATIVE SERIES TEXTS

The Cooperative Vacation Church School Texts are prepared by many denominations working together. Vacation school workers have opportunity to express the needs of their schools. The description for each course includes a statement of purpose, scope, an outline of the contents, the portions of the Bible and other resources to be used, and suggested teaching methods. These descriptions are produced cooperatively by many denominations working together in the Division of Christian Education of the National Council of the Churches of Christ in the U.S.A. The completed descriptions are approved and recommended for development into texts for use by the denominations working through the Division of Christian Education.

This cooperative process makes available to your vacation church school the best in authorship, editorial supervision, and facilities of the church publishers joining in the Cooperative Publication Association.

LIBRARY OF CONGRESS CATALOG CARD NUMBER: 62–21605

PRINTED IN THE UNITED STATES OF AMERICA

# TABLE OF CONTENTS

# foreword

While gathering material for this book, I visited churches in a variety of neighborhood situations. I found many devoted, concerned Christians leading or helping in the vacation church school programs.

There were oriental, negro, and South American mothers — some trained in teaching skills, some finding their own ways of working with the children. There were ministers' wives and seminary students from many cultural and racial backgrounds, volunteer workers from suburban churches and from established churches in city neighborhoods, and college men and women giving their summer vacations to the task of Christian education in the vacation church school.

Every teacher cried out for stories and activities to meet the special needs of inner–city children. Very few felt secure and competent in their work. Many expressed discouragement, yet without thought of giving up. They felt the children were in desperate need of what the church can give as a living, accepting, forgiving fellowship. All were willing and anxious to go on giving of themselves in the name and " in the company " of Jesus to what appeared to be an impossible task, but most of them seemed to feel they were working in the dark.

One teacher said, " Oh, I come. I'm here with them, but I don't teach them anything! "

Others protested, " They can't read. They're so restless! "

Another teacher was surprised to find the children kept coming in spite of attitudes of boredom, defiance, or at best lassitude and uncooperation. " In a way," she said, " they seem grateful, though I can't see what I'm accomplishing. I keep wanting to gather them all up and take them far, far away from this crowded, dirty, noisy, immoral place."

Another said, " We concentrate on doing for them what we can right now, with faith in God's ultimate providence for the lives of these children."

v

I saw what these teachers were doing. On the last day of the vacation church school I paraded with the children down a city street,
cleared by a policeman. All of us were carrying lunch baskets and
songbooks to a spot of green. I sang "My Hat It Has Three
Corners" in a cool church basement with a group of juniors and later
listened to them talk out fears and feelings about Russia with their
slim, young teacher. I played "Three Deep" in an empty lot at
recess time, and I heard a boy ask his teacher earnestly if it isn't all
right to love yourself "just a little bit more than you love your
neighbor." I saw a kicking, screaming child finally become calm
when a teacher held him firmly in her strong kind arms. I watched
children clear out and transform a sub-basement room to resemble
the catacombs. They were planning to have a worship service in
this room by the light of small oil lamps they had made out of clay.

Yes, I saw what these teachers were doing. They were showing
the children that the church — at least *someone* from the church —
cares about them, is interested in what they say, mourns or rejoices
about what they do, thinks enough of them to plan ahead and prepare materials for the next meeting. Yet all the time the teachers were
feeling their way, adapting materials that were adaptable and throwing out those that were not, improvising, and experimenting with
stories and activities.

In this book the resource material and the stories have been designed with inner-city children and their teachers in mind. Perhaps
reading about my experiences with the juniors in City Church will
help many of these teachers to stop floundering as I floundered at
first and get a firmer footing.

# HOW TO USE THIS BOOK

This book is designed to supplement the primary and junior vacation church school textbooks *Friends From Many Lands* and *Meet Your Neighbors*. Whether you are planning a program for primary or junior inner-city children we urge you to read this whole book. All inner-city teachers may benefit from reading the diary account of my five sessions with the children in City Church. All too may find the extra materials in the Resource Section (pages 83-118) helpful in planning for city children.

The diary is the junior section of this book (pages 1-46). It discusses five session plans adapted for inner-city juniors from the first five sessions of the junior textbook *Meet Your Neighbors*. It also contains comments of interest to inner-city teachers of other age groups.

The primary section of the book (pages 47-70) offers five session plans for use with inner-city primary children. They have been adapted from Plans 1, 3, 4, 9, and 10 of the primary textbook *Friends From Many Lands*.

Teachers of primary groups will find the primary plans more helpful after they have at least browsed through the diary in the junior section. On the other hand, teachers of juniors may find some adaptable ideas in the primary plans. Inner-city programs proceed most smoothly when alternate plans are ready to take the place of any ideas that fall flat.

If you are working with a wide age group of six- to eleven-year-olds or if you are in a section of the city where the children are extremely deprived and difficult to work with, we suggest you develop your program around the five general plans on pages 71-82. Be sure to read the diary too, and augment your program with projects and stories from either or both of the textbooks.

The vacation church school textbooks have many suggestions for helping children understand the festivals and customs of different lands and cultures. Each textbook is rich in material for acquainting children with the cultural groups represented in their own class group or for informing them about groups that are not represented in their neighborhood. But before inner-city children can concentrate on any course of study they usually need some self-understanding and a steadying relationship with a teacher who can offer love in a made-to-individual-need blend of acceptance, forgiveness, firmness, and challenge. This is to say they need a beginning experience of Christian fellowship.

The Resource Section of this book contains extra stories written with the needs and problems of inner-city children in mind. Descriptions of activities that have special appeal to the interests and abilities of these boys and girls are also included. These resources might be used to supplement vacation church school textbooks on other themes as well as the theme " The Christian and Others."

In a two-week course we suggest that the first week be spent in some such program as is outlined in one of the three sets of plans in this book. After the children have come to know each other and the teachers, after they have explored the subject of human relations in the light of Christianity, after they have experienced some friendly overtures and extended themselves in friendship to some of their fellows, perhaps in the second week they will be ready to go deeper into the study of the similarities and differences of people who come from all over the world to America.

# THE SESSION PLAN

With inner-city children session plans must be adaptable. A three-hour morning session might include:

| | |
|---|---|
| " Cafeteria " activities | Songs and games |
| Thinking and discussing | Snack |
| Purposeful work | Story |
| Bible study | Worship |

**Doodle:** " Cafeteria " activities begin the day. (See pages 9-13 for discussion of these activities.) They help the child relax and work out any tensions that may have been gathering in him. They enable him to get the feel of the group and the purposefulness of the program into his bones before he is called upon to participate in the mental aspects of it. The purposeful work of yesterday may become a " cafeteria " activity of today as the children finish or do again some of the purposeful work they may have had time only to dip into yesterday.

**Think:** Thinking and discussing can go on once emotions are under control and the feelings in the room have begun to jell rather than bubble and boil. This thinking and discussing may rise spontaneously as busy fingers are at work and the children feel free to bring up their concerns and problems or it may be stimulated and guided by a teacher who tells a story or presents a series of questions as she works with the children.

**Create:** As the children talk and think, ideas will form, and their work will move from the purposeless, tension-releasing stage into the purposeful stage. They will perhaps leave the clay or the paints or the pictures they have been talking about and go into a period of various degrees of concentration and creativity. They may work out their ideas right where they are. The projects the teacher has planned may be developed or the children may have ideas of their own to work out with materials the teacher has assembled for an entirely different purpose.

**Sing, Study, Eat, Play:** Singing may break out spontaneously as the children doodle or create. Bible study or a story may begin and enrich or culminate the thinking. Games and the juice and cookie break may be introduced to provide rest, control excitement, or to draw the group together so that the various projects and interests of the morning can be shared. All the parts of the program intertwine and supplement each other.

**Worship:** Worship climaxes the morning. The thinking and the companionship of the day are lifted and looked at in the light of God's purposes, and an effort is made to reach out for his strength, love, and guidance.

**Group responsibilities:**   Older primaries and juniors can accept some responsibility for following a schedule. Make a chart and post it where the children can see it:

## BEFORE GROUP TIME

*When you see a teacher sit down in the story corner:*
   *1. Bring some part of your work to a finish. Then lay it aside for the time being.*
   *2. Tidy up the floor and the table around you, but do not put things away until after the session. There may be time later in the morning for activities.*
   *3. Bathroom? Hands ready for the snack?*
   *4. Anyone need help? Is a friend in some difficulty with his work? Does a teacher need you for an errand?*
   *5. Take your place in the story corner.*

# SECTION 1

# diary of a junior teacher

# MONDAY

# frustration and hope

**Monday afternoon:** This might be called " The Diary of an Inexperienced, 'Experienced' Teacher " or " The Diary of a New Inner-city Teacher." Anyway, here I am at Marc Brighton's desk in City Church trying to scribble down a few details of this morning's ordeal. Marc told me to rest awhile, but these boys and girls have disturbed me too much. I don't see how I can teach them. The only successful parts of the session this morning, the only times their interest was caught and held, happened by chance, not because of my skill or preparation.

Marc has gone to get a teacher who will explain to me what he calls the " cafeteria " approach. She has had some success with it in another densely populated area. I'm too discouraged to imagine what it can be, but I'll try anything to avoid going through another morning like this one.

What happened, I wonder? I'm an experienced teacher. I taught this same course, *Meet Your Neighbors*, to the juniors in my own suburban church. They responded with enthusiasm, purposes were accomplished, and after each session I went home stimulated, not drained. How can these city boys and girls be so different?

Marc says they must be taught " in a ministering context." I wonder what he means by that. He said he would explain when he gets back here with Jean Perkins.

I don't see how I can possibly cover the material in the course with these juniors. I'll jot down some of the difficulties I had so that I can be specific when Marc and Jean arrive. Very few of the junior textbook suggestions brought favorable responses from the junior boys and girls this morning.

3

| Textbook Suggestion | Response |
|---|---|
| Sit in circle formation. | First boy took one look at circle of chairs and ran away. |
| Play get-acquainted-with-names game. | Girls giggled. Boy threw Bible behind piano. |
| Sing songs from *The Whole World Singing*. | Juniors didn't pick up tunes. Didn't even know tune of "Frère Jacques," so we couldn't sing the song about making new friends as suggested in the text. Fist fight started when I turned my back to play the piano. Marc Brighton came in and took out these boys. They didn't come back. What happened to them? |
| Have children seated and comfortable, preferably in a circle so that they may see each other as well as you and the blackboard. | They are so restless! |
| Ask, "Who are neighbors?" | "People who swipe our milk." |
| Ask, "What do you remember about the story of the good Samaritan?" | Girl who had Bible evidently knew but would not talk. |
| Discuss gestures of courtesy and friendliness for ten minutes and discuss ways in which newcomers are apt to be made to feel uncomfortable. | Afraid they would "ham" this up. Did not give them the opportunity. |
| Have children find Exodus 23:9. | Only one girl able to do this. Only one or two seem able to read readily. Time of greatest disturbance. |

Impromptu act-out skits applying ideas in Bible passages.

Not enough rapport with the group to try this. They had no Bible background to give them ideas. Wished I had arranged for one of the movies suggested in the Junior textbook (page 17). Decided to introduce handwork before recess.

Decorate cover of pupil's book with glue and sand.

First successful moments of the morning, but children not very cooperative. Could have used another teacher. Two tables with six children around each gave me too much ground to cover. These children do not work with each other in sharing tubes of glue, etc. I collected the books afterward to keep them from being destroyed. I am not sure how the children will use these pupil's books. The material seems too advanced for most of them, although they are by no means retarded. Rather, I'd call them sharply clever in undesirable ways. There are a few quiet, almost frightened girls; one black-eyed Italian boy who is cooperative and sensitive to what I am trying to do. Most of the children seem to be Puerto Ricans. There are some Negroes. I think I could work with them individually, but they certainly do not respond as a class to the methods I have used in my church at home.

Games representing different cultures during recess.

This went fairly well. I started the game " Sa Po Po " with those who finished the sand and glue work first. Then I left them and helped the others finish their work.

Sing "With Needle and Thread," and introduce pupil's book.

I was unsure by this time of my ability to hold the children's interest in anything but handwork and games. Two girls, while we were cleaning up, started to make some kind of a flower out of the pastel-colored tissues I had brought for wiping glue. I showed interest and in a very informal way the group gathered around the cleared tables again, either watching the flower-making activity or participating in it. There was plenty of material.

Explain Hawaiian welcoming custom.

I began to talk about Hawaii as suggested on page 18. I showed the children some pictures a friend had brought me of visitors being given leis. (Why does the textbook call them "ulas"?) I suggested we might make leis with the flowers they were producing in such quantities, but we didn't know how to put them together. One of the boys suggested scotch tape, but this did not hold very well and we soon ran out of our supply. Laura said her father was a tailor and she could bring us some strong thread and needles tomorrow. That would have been a good time to introduce the song "With Needle and Thread" but I didn't want to turn my back at the piano. I didn't press anyone to speak, but there was some talk about what their fathers did at work (cafe singer, hot dog man, factory worker, janitor, streetcar motorman, postal employee, dock worker).

Think about newcomers.

In this relaxed atmosphere, while the tissues were being twisted and the scotch tape was being "doodled" with, I said I was a stranger in this part of the city and asked them if they had ever felt strange and new anywhere. No response at all, but at least they were quiet.

Read the story "Abraham Welcomes Strangers."

I read the story and told them it was in the Bible too. I was about to read the verses suggested in the textbook and perhaps lead into worship, but restlessness again took over. I thought it best to collect the flowers they had made, clean up, and dismiss the group a few minutes early.

Worship together.

Evaluation questions.

Reading the evaluation questions on page 22 of *Meet Your Neighbors* makes me think I don't know how to teach at all! I do not feel I led the group this morning. I feel *they* led *me*. These children seem to have very little self-restraint. The juniors in my church can control *some* of their impulses. They don't always have to be moving or compelled by things entrancing like sand and glue or tissue paper flowers. My juniors have waited politely and silently when I've lost my page in the hymnbook or misplaced my glasses. These children slap and poke at each other and even wrestle on the floor unless something new strikes their fancy several times an hour. This was a wearying, discouraging morning.

**Monday evening:** I feel more hopeful now. Both Jean and Marc believe I can do this teaching job if I am willing to try new ways of working with these inner-city boys and girls. We talked all afternoon. I can see now that some of the material in the junior textbook will be usable if I try new methods of introducing it. I feel really adventurous!

The " cafeteria " approach and teaching in a ministering context both intrigue me. Besides, Marc said this morning was not all lost. He put the two boys who were fighting to work for him and they will be back tomorrow. He had looked in while we were having the friendly moments with tissue and scotch tape, and he said any teacher who can achieve even a few moments of such fellowship the first day is skillful enough for him. He doesn't believe they occurred without any effort of mine.

Our analysis of what happened was slightly upsetting for me. I came full of good works and good ideas and good truths I wanted to pass on to the children, but it wasn't until I accepted something from them (the idea of the tissue flowers) and revealed my sincere interest in them that I could function at all as a teacher. I must see that the children too learn that a friend and neighbor has to be willing to receive as well as give. I'm sure this idea is in the junior textbook somewhere and in other leadership materials I've read, but this morning I really learned it from experience.

Tonight I am first going to write up the " cafeteria " approach and teaching in a ministering context from the notes I took while Jean and Marc were talking. Other " experienced " teachers who are asked to work with inner-city juniors might find these ideas useful. Then I'm going to jot down some of my plans for tomorrow.

# THE *CAFETERIA* APPROACH

*(A report of my conversation with Jean Perkins)*

Inner-city children grow up in confined places. Social conditions limit their opportunity for self-fulfillment. Their family life is often unsteady and insecure. Is it any wonder that they tend to fight savagely for personal rights, seem entirely unaware of other people's needs and feelings, and clutch at material things in a vain attempt to satisfy unnamed hungers? It is any wonder that teachers find difficulty in dealing with them as a group?

The " cafeteria " approach meets this difficulty. It means laying out a tempting array of things to look at, touch, and work with so that in the beginning the teacher may be in the background, ready to help; rather than in the foreground, directing. This plan gives restless children an easier entrance to group life and work. They come into it not by being admonished to control aggressive or restless feelings and curtail individual desires and interests, but by giving vent to these in a way that does not interfere with the progress, interests, and rights of other children.

Gradually, in an atmosphere where no one pushes them and the only limits are readily understandable ones, even the most excitable children begin to see that their personal rights are not threatened if they have to wait a few minutes for their turn to speak or to do something they want very much to do. They come out from behind their defenses and become interested and cooperative in group work.

**Clay:** One of the items in a junior activity cafeteria could be clay. Use a plastic-topped table with chairs drawn up companionably around it. Have a ball of clay at each place. (A round table seems friendlier.) Impulses and feelings that would erupt into objectionable behavior when children are sitting in a circle of chairs can be frittered away harmlessly here. And after a certain amount of preliminary manipulation most juniors settle down to serious modeling.

The teacher should sympathetically put up with some nonsense — silly talk and verbal violence. Aggressive plans may be described by the boys and girls in rather gruesome language: " I'm going to get twenty steam rollers and roll you flat in the street." " I've got two thousand knives in my pocket to cut everyone up with in this many pieces." " If you put your hands around somebody's neck and squeeze and squeeze, his face gets all black and then he dies." Clay can take all this flattening and cutting up and squeezing.

If such conversation persists, a teacher may turn it into laughter by exaggerating the children's exaggerations and lifting them to a lighter plane. She may say, " I'm going to reach up and grab Mars and Venus out of the sky and play marbles with them. . . . You make me laugh so much my zygoma hurts." Teachers who can stand a little teasing, who can let a situation get a bit rowdy without allowing it to get out of hand, begin to be liked and trusted right away.

Children will try to improve their behavior if they are not threatened with impossible standards of perfection. They may show sullen dislike when a teacher does have to use her authority or strength to put a stop to some dangerously excitable behavior. But if she reveals her sadness at having to resort to the use of force or punishment and explains the trouble such behavior would lead to she will soon be forgiven. It is adults, not children, who hold grudges. This is to be remembered each day as Christian teachers begin their work. They must wipe the slate clean of the transgressions of yesterday and greet the children with expectations of nothing but complete co-operation.

Throughout all the laughter and fun one rule must hold at the clay table: *clay stays on the table.* A pan of water, paper towels, and a wastebasket nearby can be pointed to by a teacher who says good-naturedly, " Tom, our fun will turn to trouble if you throw clay. If you are not interested here you may clean the clay off your hands and go to some other table."

After the children have manipulated the clay awhile for fun, their teacher may say, " I see some of you are beginning to get the feel of this clay. Mary and Pete are using their thoughts as well as their hands as they work." (Tomorrow I may show the pictures of the Statue of Liberty and Thorwaldsen's statue of Christ in the junior pupil's book and say, " The Statue of Liberty is an idea worked out in a model. Can you think of any other way to express the idea of freedom and welcome? ")

Jean helped me to see that all the discussions suggested in Session 2 of the junior textbook might well be carried on around a clay table. Strangers can get to know each other. Newcomers are accepted here. A clay table does for children what tea parties and coffee breaks do for adults.

**Easel painting:** Item number two in the cafeteria of activities could be big sheets of paper, long brushes, and poster paint. If stand-up easels are not available, the paper may be laid out on a long table where at least three children can work at one time.

Painting, like clay, is sometimes just fun. Other times, as the bright colors flow so smoothly on the paper, tongues are freed, bewilderments expressed, and heavy hearts unburdened. The pictures will probably be largely a painting-out of feelings — gay, sad, mixed-up — and the children may paint one picture after another with great satisfaction. Jean says that an adult hovering in the background should muse: Who has loved this child? How has this one been frightened? Did these sisters have breakfast today? Where has this boy heard of God? Teachers get to know the children as they paint.

When a child can't control himself enough in a group discussion to let someone else talk, he may quiet down if he is allowed to stand at an easel on the fringe of the group and paint while the others are talking and listening. If you watch such a child you realize that he continues to participate in the discussion by expressing himself in colors on paper. Fringe painters listen to a story too. Sometimes they illustrate it specifically, sometimes they reveal the story's emotional tone. Perhaps later on the painter can be persuaded to tell a teacher or the whole group about his paintings and so find a means of belonging to the fellowship.

The cafeteria idea, thus, is helpful throughout the session, not only as the children come in. It is too much to expect of inner-city children, Jean reminded me, that they all do the same thing at the same time. Being able to make choices gives the boys and girls enough of a feeling of freedom to keep at a minimum those outbursts and rebellious moments when a teacher has to put her foot down to keep order.

**Sand and glue activities:** A third cafeteria item for the first few days could be a sand and glue table. (This will continue the activity begun today when the children decorated the letters on the covers of the pupil's books.) Name tags could be made and the letters decorated. Perhaps the name of the church and of the group could be added. Pictures cut from magazines or painted by the children might be mounted on colored paper, and sand and glue borders put around them. Appropriate pictures may be hung in the worship center, others may be used for gifts.

**Tissue flowers:** Jean congratulated me on picking up the children's interest in the tissue flowers. The making of the flowers and leis may continue at another table.

**Art activities:** Colored paper, crayons, scissors, paste, and a clear space to work in are treasures to most inner-city children. They could provide another cafeteria activity.

Unlike clay and easel painting, work with sand and glue, the making of tissue flowers and — usually — the paper, scissors, and paste activity are purposeful from the start.

**Use of pictures:** The cafeteria approach should go beyond the activity period. The teacher needs a variety of approaches to problems and needs that arise throughout the session. A series of pictures might be mounted on the wall in an area apart from the activity table: pictures of a child being scolded, a boy with a bat near a broken window, a girl resplendent in finery, a girl sitting alone on a doorstep, a small boy chasing a big boy, or a big boy chasing a small boy. Such pictures help boys and girls to talk. Children who interrupt worshipful moments may be led here by a teacher to talk out their feelings. She may just listen, or she may ask: " How do you think the boy in this picture feels? What would you say this girl is thinking? " Then later she may ask: " How do you think the children feel when they want to sing and you keep stamping your feet? "

**Handling strong feelings:** In the inner city a teacher must always be ready to deal with strong feelings. A real punching bag or a football dummy installed somewhere not too far from the classroom may help a child learn that angers don't always have to be worked out on people. If two boys are bound and determined to fight it out, give them each a bat made of a rolled newspaper. Two or three swats and the weapons are usually as limp as the angry feelings. Some of the most active games suggested in the junior textbook help to blow off steam too — " The Big Snake " (page 136) or " Tug " (page 140).

There are ways to help disturbing children develop acceptable behavior patterns. These methods are the same everywhere. Someone must show individual care for each disturber. He is not to be one-fifteenth of a class, not just another difficult-to-deal-with person;

but a valued person, worthy of respect and understanding. After some friendly teacher-child relationships have been established by means of the cafeteria approach, Jean told me, the foundation is laid for the kind of discussions and story and worship periods I have been accustomed to in working with children in a more favorable area.

All this special attention calls for extra adult help. A program with inner-city children is very difficult if there are not enough alert, sympathetic adult friends around to do some personal work while one teacher is working with the group. (I asked Marc to try to get me a couple of assistants.) But, Jean concluded, no matter what you do there may be times when the only way to get the attention of some children would be to show them something as unusual as a dead dinosaur in a little box!

# TEACHING IN A MINISTERING CONTEXT

*(A report of my conversation with Marc Brighton)*

In communities where the living is pleasant and family life fairly stable, children usually come to school and church ripe and eager for learning. They have known gentleness, understanding, unselfishness, and concern. They are ready to think about these ennobling human traits and, under guidance, to begin practicing them. A teacher can count upon their past experiences to enrich class discussions about friendliness or neighborliness.

Most of these children can understand that God is a loving, forgiving father because they have loving, forgiving human fathers around them. They can understand Jesus' teachings about God's care and concern because they see illustrations of it in the birds, trees, flowers, and grass that are part of their daily experiences. They are ready for information that will enrich their experiences and help them grow in Christian knowledge.

Teachers in these communities don't have to feel their way. They can use material in textbooks, making only slight adaptations to meet individual needs.

**Problems we face:** Teaching in inner-city church schools is more difficult. Decaying buildings, junk-filled vacant lots, and treeless, grassless stretches of concrete give children no hint of God's creative activity and sustaining love and care.

Inner-city children come from a variety of circumstances. Teachers cannot bank upon helpful preparatory experiences in the lives of these pupils. They usually have to work against a background of unhelpful experiences. Some boys and girls come from fatherless homes. Others come to the church skeptical and rebellious. Before they are ten years old some have brushed up against or even participated in greed, brutality, and ruthlessness. At the other extreme are the ones who have been carefully sheltered and trained into rigid morality by strict parents desperately wanting their children to have a better life. Other parents may have been too preoccupied with living and working troubles to do more than sink into restful apathy at home, and their children have had little or no guidance as they grew.

We should be sympathetic to the parents, rather than critical of those who seem to be unable to bestir themselves to better their living conditions. An analysis of economic conditions would reveal to us causes for the unlovely way of life largely prevalent in the inner city.

Of course there are areas in the city where children experience just as much graciousness as greed. A detailed account of life, even in the most congested districts, would show God's love breaking through in seemingly hopeless conditions, revealing itself here and there in family devotion, in good-hearted companionship, or in quiet unselfishness.

**Our task:** We should give praise to God for the wonders he performs in spite of the obstacles people put in his way. We should support and advocate social and economic programs that will make inner-city life more hopeful. We must, however, also keep in mind the most deprived inner-city children and concern ourselves with helping God's love break through more often for them.

Inner-city children need to have an experience of the kind of strong, growth-producing love that Jesus showed. It is up to us to make the effort to welcome human souls into fellowship, to help them feel the dignity and personal worth that is their birthright, to lead them into desirable achievement, and to foster the development of their best capabilities without violating the rights of others but by *aiding* others in similar personal development.

**Ministering to needs:** Seen in this light our simplest words of welcome may be meaningful. The mundane tasks we do to get ready for a session will be almost sacramental. And the activity periods will be full of precious opportunities for helping the children discover and develop values in themselves and others and gain insight into God's plan for loving relationships — God with man, and man with man. This is what is meant by teaching in a ministering context.

Yet unless we do all these common tasks in the company of Jesus, unless we seek God's help and his glory as we serve, our work may indeed be just directing an off-the-street club. No real and continuing progress can be achieved unless we have opened ourselves to the grace of God.

# ADVICE FROM
# EXPERIENCED TEACHERS

My head is awhirl, but as I practice all the advice I got this afternoon I'm sure it will all make sense and help me to do what I want to do for my inner-city juniors. Other teachers came in while I was sitting in Marc's office. They wanted to know how my morning went and were most sympathetic with my problems. Each one offered some helpful advice and suggestions. I must jot these down to help me remember and to pass on the hints to other teachers.

**Self-government:** Don't attempt pupil-governed groups and pupil-planned projects until you know your children, advised several teachers. In more favored neighborhoods democratic practices can be profitably introduced when the desire for clubs of their own arises in children. But inner-city children must first learn give-and-take, respect for others' rights and needs, and some self-discipline before these privileges can be granted.

**Why children fight:** There are eight hundred and ninety-nine reasons why a fist fight will interrupt the first five minutes of even the discussion on welcoming procedures (such as suggested on page 11 of the junior text). Among these reasons are: unacquaintance with self-restraint, excitability because of improper food or lack of sleep, admonishings to guard personal rights feverishly, unawareness of the rights of others, pent-up hostility due to an ever-present feeling of rejection which is vented upon even closest friends at the least provocation. On the first day of school inner-city children need a welcoming *experience*, rather than a discussion about it.

**Using the Bible:** Bible study periods must be worked up to gradually. The prevailing attitudes toward education in general are negative. The children seem to feel that no matter how much they learn they will never be completely accepted, so why not spend time in other pursuits that will pay off more quickly? Many of the inner-city boys and girls have no Bible background at all: no experiences with hills, trees, and lakes to make biblical geography and references significant. Some of them have already been introduced to and rejected the Bible as a white man's book with an Anglo-Saxon Jesus. The biblical content listed in the vacation church school textbooks is excellently chosen, but inner-city teachers have to find new and unique ways of presenting it. They have to spend time and trouble setting up situations in which learning can take place.

**Rules and discipline:** Standards of order and discipline need to be flexible and within the children's understanding. Games requiring turns should be avoided at first. Once a relationship has been established between a child and a teacher, disciplining by withdrawal of love is extremely detrimental. Adults must be prepared to take a great deal of testing in their relationships with the children.

# TUESDAY

# a welcome for all

*(Adaptation of Session 2, Junior Textbook)*

## ROOM ARRANGEMENT

If I'm going to rearrange the room for cafeteria activities, I will have to be there early. Marc said people from cooperating churches will bring in easels and painting supplies, but I haven't decided yet in what part of the room they will be most convenient. I should mix the paint myself tomorrow, then I can teach the juniors how to do it.

The two neighborhood mothers whom Marc has recruited to work with me can help me put some adhesive-backed plastic on the clay table while we are talking about plans for the session. Marc said there is a drum of clay in the church, but we will have to have plastic bags or a crock in which to store it.

We'll put the clay table near the door, the easels under the windows, I think. The sand and glue table and the place where the children may work with tissues and make leis will be on the opposite side of the room. The gathering place will be in the alcove.

Tomorrow the gathering place will *not* be a circle of chairs. There is a long, sturdy oak table along the wall near one corner. I imagine those three tall boys would like to sit on it and swing their legs while we talk or sing together. I remember seeing a low bench somewhere in the church and some campstools. These can be set up by the boys and girls themselves in an informal way.

The same area may be set up more formally for worship periods as we plan them together. I'll bring marigolds from my garden. Some of the girls may want to arrange them for this worship center. My picture file will need a going-over, but I'm sure there is some material in it that will reflect the problems and wonderings of these boys and girls and so inspire thoughtful and worshipful moments.

On the other hand, I must remember that probably most of the discussing and singing will go on in the small groups around the activity centers. We may not use this gathering place tomorrow except for a few moments after recess when we have our juice and cookies. (These I have decided will both help the undernourished children and help me hold attention while I read the story.) Of course, if all goes as well as I hope it will, most of the children will gather there at the end of the morning for worship.

# PURPOSE

The junior textbook builds the second session around the idea of the American tradition of welcoming strangers which stems in large measure from our Judeo-Christian heritage.

As a newcomer to this church I feel a little strange and uncomfortable myself. I suppose the juniors felt the same way yesterday. In my own church it has always seemed easy to establish rapport with new pupils, so I didn't realize a teacher might have to really work to make newcomers feel welcome. Tomorrow I shall be more sensitive to feelings and less anxious about covering the material. In a very childish way I was more concerned in the first session about my own feelings, chagrin and embarrassment because things did not go the way I had expected them to go, than I was about the children's feelings. Perhaps we can make a new beginning from our good moments of yesterday when the girls made flowers, the boys tried to tie them together into leis, and Laura offered to bring needles and thread.

*My purpose for the session, therefore, will be to help the children feel like much-wanted newcomers who really belong in the church.* I — that should be *we*, now that I have two helpers — shall try to tie this feeling in with the two concepts the junior textbook introduces: America's tradition of welcoming strangers as illustrated in the Statue of Liberty, and the source of this tradition in the Judeo-Christian heritage as illustrated in Thorwaldsen's statue of Christ.

# BIBLE

Jesus' invitation to the weary to come unto him (Matthew 11: 28), and the first part of the parable of the last judgment (Matthew 25:35-40) will tie in with any talk about the statues and therefore be easy for our pupils to understand. The country story in the book of Ruth and the ancient laws of sharing the harvest (Deuteronomy 24:19-20) suggested for use with this session might widen the horizons of these city children but would be more difficult to relate to their lives. The offer of free mercy to all (Isaiah 55:1) might also be interpreted in conversation about the statues.

# MATERIALS

**Cafeteria activities:** Clay, paints, tissues, bobby pins, sand, glue

**Pupil's books:** (For pictures of the statues; also for the words to the song " Thomas Jefferski " on page 43)

**Hymns:** (from *Hymns for Junior Worship*) " America the Beautiful," No. 108; " Our City," No. 109 (I can sing " America the Beautiful " without the piano, if need be, and we can read the words to " Our City " prayerfully as the junior textbook suggests.)

**Group activities:** Blackboard or brown paper for class family tree; United Nations Flag Chart [Available from the Sales Section, United Nations, New York; thirty cents. Orders must be prepaid.]

# CHECK OF TEXTBOOK SUGGESTIONS

1. We'll postpone or leave out the radio broadcast because it requires so much reading.

2. We'll postpone the making of felt pennants and handkerchiefs for a while because such work does not aid the release of troublesome and excitable feelings as clay work and painting do.

3. American and Christian flags are in the sanctuary. One day during these two weeks we shall go there for our worship, but not before we have had some experiences of reverence and awe in our own room. Until I know which boys and girls can read without

embarrassment we shall postpone such procedures as preparing cards with statements on them to be read during worship.

4. We'll sing without the piano unless one of the neighborhood mothers can play. I might say the words of " America the Beautiful " while the children hum or perhaps whistle the tune.

5. We'll make the class family tree on brown paper with crayola and flags. We have an Italian boy. Linda, I think, may be Lithuanian; Enrico, Puerto Rican; Ramon, Mexican. . . .

6. For games, I think we'll play " Sa Po Po " again and perhaps " The Big Snake " (pages 141 and 136, junior textbook).

7. I'll read the story about names myself. There won't be time to practice reading it dramatically with the new teachers. I want to spend the half hour I have with them before the session talking about the purpose as I have described it above and about subject matter to introduce as the children work with clay, paint and other materials.

8. I'll wait one more day to introduce the picture dictionary project. We may leave this out.

9. Perhaps we'll have a record player later in the week to help with the singing.

10. My two mother-teachers may know people in the neighborhood whom the children could interview for the Wednesday session.

11. No scavenger hunt. We may collect things, but not during class hours. We need to spend more time together.

*Note:* See Marc about getting a sound projector or a record player so that we can use the movie or records suggested in the junior textbook (page 23) to help the singing along. Perhaps around the tables tomorrow the boys and girls will sing some of the songs they already know — if I am as receptive about the songs as I was about the tissue flowers.

# SCHEDULE

I'm not going to break the session into as many parts as those suggested in the junior textbook. That was what troubled me yesterday. I could see the time going by and nothing (I thought) being accomplished towards the purpose.

**8:45:**   Cafeteria activities
Small group discussions
Singing

**10:15:**  Tidy up (leaving unfinished work out for the children who get restless during group time)
Wash hands
Games

**10:30:**  Juice and cookies
Story about names
Class family tree
Names in telephone book
Song, " Thomas Jefferski "
(Gradually restless children will be allowed to go back to table work. Helping teachers will go with them.)

**11:30:**  Plan worship (I shall remain with interested children to do this planning.)

**11:45:**  Put things away and come to gathering place
Worship

**Cafeteria activities:** In the beginning there should be a welcoming adult (who will supervise too) in each section of the room. Every child can find something to do of his own choosing, or a teacher can talk with him and find out why he is not interested in these activities that his friends accept so readily. After a while (and gradually) the teacher at each table should try to introduce conversation about the Statue of Liberty, first discovering what the children know about this statue and what it stands for, then adding information to the children's store of knowledge about it.

Perhaps some will want to paint or model their own statues, either now or after they have delved into the biblical ideas which may have inspired both Lazarus and Thorwaldsen.

As far as possible at this time the teachers in each group will pursue the conversations about the meaning of the Statue of Liberty, reasons why people have moved to America (religious freedom, adventure, social or economic improvement, escape from tyranny) and the problems or disappointments they faced, how newcomers learn to get along with people who have lived here a longer time. (Follow suggestions for these discussions on pages 25, 28, and 29, in junior textbook; also ways to bring in Bible study, page 30.)

Restless children must be allowed to move from group to group, but if a child is definitely disturbing, I shall deal with him personally. I'll point out that by this time the others have found some satisfying activity and try to help him understand what keeps him from doing so. Perhaps he has something on his mind he would like to talk out. Perhaps he doesn't feel the children around the table are his friends. Is there anyone here who is in his class at school? Who lives on his block? Who is as tall as he is?

During this period I hope a group of the children will break into spontaneous singing of " America the Beautiful " or some folk song they know and can help us all to learn.

**Transition:** At 10:15 the teachers will begin to excuse children to go to the washroom, tidying up the room first, but leaving work out. I'll start games with those who are ready first. Some girls may want to help a teacher prepare the juice and cookie treat at this time.

**Group time:** After everyone has moved around a bit we'll find comfortable places to sit in the gathering place. I'll tell them that I am accustomed to speaking or singing my thanks to God before I eat and ask them to be quiet while I pray: " Thank you, God, for the acts of friendliness and helpfulness we have seen here this morning and for this treat of juice and cookies which we are about to enjoy together. Amen."

Rather than put up with too much disturbance during the story, the class family-tree discussion, the telephone book reading, and the song, " Thomas Jefferski," I shall ask the children who become restless to leave with a teacher. They may mount and frame a picture for our worship period or return to the work they have started earlier or try something new in the way of activities. By 11:30 I should have around me only the boys and girls interested in planning a worship service for the group.

These children may have their own ideas about worship. Or the service could be only a quiet moment before a picture of Jesus, centered between the sand-and-glue-framed statue pictures from the junior pupil's book. I might read the Bible selection that was most talked about and read the hymn, " Our City," as a prayer.

Now to bed with much gratefulness to God who so richly provides resources for teachers who suddenly discover their inadequacies.

# TUESDAY NIGHT

Tonight I can face the evaluation questions on page 22 in the junior textbook. The time schedule was just about right as I had revised it. The children participated at various levels of concentration and interest. I felt a change in attitude toward me and the whole program today.

All the boys and girls still protect their own rights much more vigorously than those of their friends, but there was some cooperation. We seem to be successful in helping the children control their angers or at least release them in harmless activity. Anyway, no fist fights broke out today. Two boys need personal attention almost all the time and several of the girls are still not quite at ease, but we can deal with these problems now that Maria and Rosa are working with me. Bible study is entirely new to five children. The others are interested enough — with teacher guidance.

There is a nucleus of thinkers and planners in the group. As I suspected, these are the children who stayed with me at story time and afterwards to talk about worship. The arrangement I have made with Maria and Rosa provides for the sliding scale of attention spans by allowing restless children to get up and work at the tables as their interest in the discussion or story wanes. I believe it will increase capacities for group participation by the end of the week. Two children who left the group today came back when laughter broke out while we were making our class family tree.

My worship ideas were accepted by the planners almost verbatim, but we did discuss worship. They set up the pictures and read the Bible verse and prayer. We all sang, "He's Got the Whole World in His Hands," because the planners said all the children knew it. And they did.

I should have liked it better if these children had arranged the whole worship service as my juniors at home do, but I have noted in reading about the characteristics of nine- to eleven-year-olds that during this period most children tend to take unto themselves the ideas and values of adults who are important in their lives. So I am feeling important — and very humble.

# HOME INFLUENCES IN THE INNER CITY

Rosa and I visited the homes of some of the children today. Rosa was very patient with me.

" Why do these people buy a new television set when they can't even afford a flat with its own bathroom? " I wanted to know.

Rosa said, " Otherwise the father and older brother might spend every night in a tavern."

I asked, " Don't these people ever give the children anything to eat but pork and beans and potato chips? "

Rosa explained, " You know how hot it is in those flats. To cook, to light the gas stove for even ten minutes, makes it worse. In the summer here we all try not to cook."

As we went up and down the streets and through the hallways I kept wondering what we would find behind the next door. Behind one was a mother whose warmth and tenderness with her children enriched their lives more than thick rugs and fine furniture ever could. Behind another was a family that made our hearts sing with hope as they talked about their patient plans to raise their living standards.

I began to understand why Calo taunts Alex when I discovered that at home he has been taught to scorn Alex's whole family. Rosa says that people who bestir themselves to better their own living conditions are sometimes very hard on members of their own race who don't have the ambition to do this.

As the afternoon wore on, my dress became limp and grimy with city soot. I began to see why parents try to maintain a semblance of neatness by decking their children out in more shiny new shoes and bright new clothes than I have seen in other areas where parents can more easily afford them.

Rosa told me not to be surprised at the luxurious furnishings I would find in some run-down houses. She said, " These families work hard and save their money. They would like to live somewhere else, but they can't find a landlord who will let them rent in any other neighborhood. So they make the best home they can here for their children." I could see how families that had scrimped and saved for years to be able to move into a better neighborhood, only to find they would not be accepted there, might settle for material satisfactions of the present moment. In resignation parents might pamper their children with money for corner-store trinkets and candy when the greatest need appeared to be for dental work.

These children I teach and their parents have made me aware of the problems of inner-city families. I cannot approve of some of their ways, but Rosa's sympathetic understanding has kept me from being completely baffled by the inconsistencies of their lives. I wish I could wave a magic wand to better economic conditions, provide legal action to prevent exploitation, and improve health habits and sanitation. At least I know there are people working to do this, but it will take time. Meanwhile I must work with conditions as they are, help where I can, and try to understand.

How can I bolster the moral strength and courage of these people to help them meet the frustrations that beset them? How better than by ministering to them as wholeheartedly as I can in the name and in the company of Jesus? Rosa and Maria live here and their lives are triumphant. It is the acceptance and understanding of God's love that makes all the difference. I will try to show my pupils and their families my respect and concern and hopes for them.

# WEDNESDAY

# gifts of many kinds

*(Adaptation of Session 3, Junior Textbook)*

## PLANNING AHEAD

By Friday of this week we should feel close enough to the boys and girls to have them invite their families to an open house at church. Maybe we could move our " cafeteria " into the big hall of the church and let the children, who are in the know, serve as hosts and guides while the guests paint, work with clay or sand and glue, sing, hear a story, and worship together.

But tomorrow is Wednesday, not Friday, and I must adapt the session " Richer by Others " to our special needs.

## PURPOSE

Just as America has been made richer by the contributions of other cultures, so have individual people been helped by acts of Christian love and friendliness such as we wish to inspire in our juniors. These inner-city children may not be aware of how their lives have been made richer by others, of how much love they have received. Acts of friendliness may have been unnoticed. *Our purpose for this session will be to open the eyes of the children to the contributions*

27

*of people either to our culture or to our individual needs.* Perhaps we can help them begin to realize that they can enrich the lives of others with friendship and love.

# BIBLE

The Bible selections suggested for this session are difficult for juniors to understand. Still, Paul's discourses on the different abilities of different people (Romans 12:3-10 and 1 Corinthians 12:4-31) will be helpful in ministering to the special needs of these children. At least it helps us as teachers not to expect the same growth or performance from them all. They seem to have a desperate need for a sense of adequacy and achievement. I was so glad to see Rosa and Maria beaming in unmistakable awe at the children's pictures and modelings.

In interpreting this Bible selection, and indeed all through the morning, I must help the children discover qualities and abilities in themselves that they may not be aware of. I must help them see God's power at work in us all and in the world about us.

They may have difficulty finding and reading Bible passages, but when we plan worship I'm going to help them find and read Paul's writings about love in 1 Corinthians 13. Just because many of these boys and girls can't read readily is no reason to skip reading entirely. During this period in their lives reading efficiency should increase rapidly. All we need is patience to keep our expectations only a little beyond their present ability, not so far beyond as to make them give up trying. The words in the *Revised Standard Version of the Bible* are quite clear, but before we read I shall write words such as *gong, cymbals, prophetic, irritable, arrogant* and others on the board and explain them.

# MATERIALS

All activity materials are on hand from this morning except a film projector which will come Thursday, and neon paint which we won't use anyway. The picture to be painted in the pupil's book is detailed and precise. I believe these children will do better in less exacting work at present. There is a roll of shelf paper and some dowel sticks in the cupboard. If some of the boys and girls want they may make illustrations of a story, attach them to the shelf paper and roll it scroll-wise on the sticks à la the paper theater activity on page 44 of the junior textbook.

As for hymns and songs, we do better with those the children know already. There was some singing and whistling around the tables this morning, but I had to solo "America the Beautiful." Rosa is going to ask her cousin to bring her guitar tomorrow. We may be able to add a music corner to our cafeteria and have an informal singing group there while other children are working with clay, painting, or making a paper theater.

# CHECK OF TEXTBOOK SUGGESTIONS

1. We shall certainly keep any things the children bring to illustrate cultural contributions until Friday night, at least, so that the parents may see them. I must appoint a junior to pack them carefully after each session and store them in the church office until Friday. In this neighborhood it may be best not to leave out tempting things.

2. No walking trip. I don't feel close enough to the children yet to be sure they would stay with me away from the church.

3. Rosa and Maria are warm-hearted women who love the children, listen to them, help them, and keep order. But they have not taught before and haven't had time to become familiar with the course. I can see, therefore, that I'm the one who will have to stimulate discussions and challenge the children to create, cooperate with each other on special projects, and in general participate at the height of their respective abilities. This morning I was a table hopper. I went from clay to paints to sand and glue with the Bible and the pictures of the Statue of Liberty and Thorwaldsen's statue of Christ. Evidently I stimulated some serious thought because by recess time there was a painting of an open door and a clay model of City Church complete with the cross on top. The creator of each said his production expressed the idea of welcome.

4. Planning for a final session and committees working now to prepare a special program for it would be too big a job for this

group. We'll stick to the idea of an open house on Friday when the parents will be able to see — and try — what the children are doing these mornings. Tomorrow after recess I'll ask the children how to invite their families. Perhaps paper tickets could be made, one for each guest. The children could print the time and the place on them. This shouldn't be too much work for part of the group to do while others are planning the worship.

5. I have the songbook, *Little Songs on Big Subjects*. [See bibliography, page 118.] Perhaps Rosa's cousin will be able to introduce some of these songs with her guitar. She doesn't have to turn her back to the children to play it. Since chords are marked in this book perhaps I can try them on an Autoharp or ukelele and sing with the children myself without turning my back.

# SCHEDULE

**Cafeteria activities (8:45-10:15):** Use the ones laid out yesterday plus singing with Rosa's cousin in the gathering place.

We may make a paper theater, but the project will not be developed just as described in the junior textbook, page 44. While the children work around the clay table and at the easels we'll read the stories about Juan (see pages 88-92 in the Resource Section of this book) who lived in the city and wondered constantly what a friend is. These stories, I hope, will spark conversation about friendly acts the children have seen or experienced. Clay modelings, paintings, or a paper theater can then be made to illustrate what has been talked about or to illustrate the stories.

Later all these might be used in worship. For instance, if several children have produced items that portray friendliness, they might show them and tell about them in turn. After each showing the whole group might say, as in a litany: "We give thanks to you, O God, that people can show friendliness to each other."

**Transition (10:15):** Cleanup, recess, games as yesterday

**Group time (10:30):** Begin with a brief discussion about how to invite the parents to the open house on Friday night. Show of hands as to who will plan the worship after this period and who will make invitations or tickets.

At this time we'll have Maria and Rosa's contributions. My two neighborhood teachers did not know any people we could interview for the Wednesday session about cultural contributions from other countries. I think they were reluctant to put their neighbors on the spot to do something that might embarrass them. So Maria and Rosa themselves are going to be interviewed. Maria will tell how birthdays were celebrated in Czechoslovakia and bring the treat — and the recipe for it. Rosa will tell about her church in Puerto Rico and say grace for us in her native language.

After that we'll call attention to contributions made by people of various lands and races: Pasteur's (French) work to make milk safe to drink; George Washington Carver's (Negro) development of paint, oil, and other products from peanuts; Joe Di Maggio's (Italian) contribution to sports; Dr. Jonas Salk's (Jewish) discovery of polio vaccine. Then we will challenge the children to discover in their neighborhood interesting people and things from other countries. We will suggest that they look at trademarks on their toys, clothes, and kitchenware to see if they have anything that was made in another country. They might make a list of the shops in their neighborhood to find out how many different countries and races are represented there. (Check pages 42 and 43 of the junior textbook for other ideas.) I shall also read the scavenger hunt list (page 41) to give them more ideas about things for which they may look.

**Committee work (11:00 or 11:15):** Talking about the Bible passages and interpreting them should lead into planning the worship and making the tickets or invitations. Or some boys and girls may need releasing clay work and painting again. If a paper theater was started the children may need this time to finish it.

**Worship (11:45):** The worship should include a reading of 1 Corinthians 13, a showing of meaningful work, and recognition of the contributions made by Maria and Rosa — and Laura, who helpfully brought sewing materials for the leis.

The juniors who plan the worship might read together the prayer on page 48 in the junior textbook and write it in their own words. Perhaps, since the children are slow in learning hymns, Rosa's cousin will close our worship with some meditative strumming on her guitar as we hum one of the hymn tunes.

# WEDNESDAY NIGHT

The time schedule is just right now. Our mornings are taking shape and the children know what to expect. Most of them seem to enjoy the free clay and paint work, but are ready to listen when I come with a story as it may lead to a discussion that will give them some definite plans and ideas to work out.

Of course Calo and Alex, the two boys that Marc took out of the room the first day, need constant supervision. They have not yet found themselves in any activity, nor does the clay or paint release them enough so that they can participate in the more purposeful work the other children are enjoying.

This morning several committees were formed: one to make a paper theater, another to paint pictures about friendly acts for it, another to make very fancy tickets decorated with sand and glue.

Maria's treat, Rosa's grace, and her cousin's music were thought about silently at the beginning of the worship period. One by one attention was called to these contributions. Then Millie read 1 Corinthians 12: 4-11 and announced the worship committee's thought for the day: " All people have different talents, but everyone can do some kind of friendly act." (The discussion never moved to a point where I could meaningfully introduce 1 Corinthians 13.)

The prayer on page 48 in the junior textbook was read verbatim and the group sang " He's Got the Whole World in His Hands " with guitar accompaniment.

# THURSDAY

# we're all different

*(Adaptation of Session 4, Junior Textbook)*

Our program is streamlined each day to the simplest, briefest form, but it is meaningful to our inner-city children. We seem to be working and playing together with increasing friendliness — all except Calo and Alex.

Calo has finally realized that I mean it when I say, "Clay stays on the table." He now sits down and lifts a big lump as high as he can and crashes it down on the table with a terrible bang. "It's a bomb," he says.

I sat next to him for a while today. After the first crash he looked at me sideways and said, "You got all burned up that time."

I agreed with him quietly, "I was all burned up that time," and continued to sit there in a reassuring state of perfect health. I am not a psychologist, but I know we are all full of fears and unexplored feelings. If Calo needs to work out the bomb idea and involves me because I restrain him and won't let him bulldoze his wild way through this group, then I'll let him relieve his angers against me with the unhurtable clay.

When he tired of fire-bomb play, he announced that the clay was a parachute. His plane was burning and he was riding down in the parachute to safety. Will the day ever come, I wonder, when he takes me along with him in the parachute?

33

Calo might look upon me as a friend if I could help him accomplish something that would make the other children look at him with something besides fear or disdain. I have watched the children and that is the way they do regard him — probably because he has done nothing but disrupt work, tease, and actually hurt some children.

Except for Calo and Alex the children seem to be finding satisfaction of some kind in our program. Most of them are, in some sense at least, considerate of and friendly with others. It is certainly true that we find fulfillment for ourselves as we relate in sympathetic understanding and giving to other people. I suppose this is one of the things Jesus meant when he said that he who loses his life shall find it. Most of these boys and girls beam and glow when they have produced a picture they can talk about, one that interests the other children because it illustrates a point we have been discussing. Some have a contented look after merely sponging off the clay table.

Calo and Alex never beam or glow or look contented. The only good trait I have noticed in them is a kind of loyalty they have for each other. When Marc came in Monday as they were grappling on the floor he took Calo (who happened to be on top) and lifted him bodily out of the room, Alex immediately transferred his hostility to Marc, pounding him as he walked away and yelling some words I don't care to repeat. The essence of what he said was, " Where ya takin' him? He didn't do nuthin '. " And of course he followed his enemy-friend out of the room.

Perhaps I can strengthen this feeling they have for each other and help them extend it to take in other children, even the teachers. It may be that all their lives these two boys have been scolded, stopped from doing what they wanted to do, kept from having what they felt they needed. They are now nine years old and act like kindergarten children.

Well, I've described the problem. Now to think of some ways to work on it:

1. Help them find some satisfying thing to do, something they can do well, something that will give them status in the eyes of the other children.

2. Help them contribute something to this group or somehow feel they really belong to it.

If we can help them in these two ways, I believe they may begin to grow out of their aggressive and damaging behavior into more acceptable patterns of relating to others.

# PURPOSE

The purpose suggested for Session 4 in the junior textbook is threefold: to introduce something of the origin of various racial or national groups; to help juniors understand that behavior is determined by where we live and how we are brought up, not by blood or skin color; and to guide children's thinking about God the creator who gave each of us different gifts and abilities and who loves all the people he has created and wants us to love them too.

In the textbook statement of purpose *behavior* refers to cultural customs that may be ridiculed and misunderstood, not to objectionable and anti-social behavior. Nevertheless, I believe that all behavior has a cause behind it whether it be cultural custom or personal action. Understanding the cause makes it possible to accept or change the behavior as the need may be. I know I should probably be acting up the way Calo and Alex are if I had been brought up here in the inner city in their particular family groups.

*Our adaptation of the purpose for this session will be to help the children understand that God has created men different and that we should accept our differences as God-given assets, not as reasons for alienation or division.*

Again I think of Calo and Alex. Their behavior tends to alienate me from them. It is only by making a supreme effort to understand them that I can find ways of working with them as a teacher. Certainly their behavior does not seem to be a God-given asset — or is it? They have verve and vigor and spirit and great big grins. Perhaps it is a matter of turning all this life into useful, rather than damaging, channels.

# BIBLE

My group of juniors at home studied all the Bible selections listed on page 49 in the junior textbook after dramatizing the "Biggle-Gog" story on page 53. I'm not sure how much of this Bible work we can do tomorrow.

Behold, how good and pleasant it is
when brothers dwell in unity!

— Psalm 133:1

The Lord is good to all,
> and his compassion is over all that he has
>> made.

> — Psalm 145:9

So far so good, but the selection from Zechariah (7:8-14) gives the Old Testament picture of a God of laws and of wrath for those who don't obey the laws. I think these children have not yet known God well enough as Jesus pictured him — as a loving father requiring greatness of us, yet offering forgiveness and understanding as well as orders. We shall skip this reference.

Peter's thoughts of God are usually helpful: "Truly I perceive that God shows no partiality, but in every nation any one who fears him and does what is right is acceptable to him" (Acts 10:34a-35). Still . . . "fears him." I believe our inner-city juniors need more experience of the unmerited, unconditional love that Jesus gave so freely before they come to grips with the demands he made. These Bible verses taken out of context can teach the very opposite of what we intend. How important it is for a teacher, especially in an inner-city situation, to teach out of her total understanding of Christianity and God's love; rather than expect isolated Bible verses to preach the gospel for her. Help me, help us all, God, to do this.

Acts 17:24-27 is not so threatening: "The God who made the world and everything in it, being Lord of heaven and earth, does not live in shrines made by man, nor is he served by human hands, as though he needed anything, since he himself gives to all men life and breath and everything. And he made from one every nation of men to live on all the face of the earth, having determined allotted periods and the boundaries of their habitation, that they should seek God, in the hope that they might feel after him and find him. Yet he is not far from each one of us."

We have to live and love and suffer as much as Paul did, I suppose, before we can realize that it is only by God's help that we even reach out to him. This is a deep, involved thought, but in these verses Paul does portray God in his majesty and yet shows his availability too. I wonder what the children will understand of this.

Galatians 3:28 and Colossians 3:11 will have to be translated very freely in order for our boys and girls to understand them. Just as they are beginning to establish their identity as persons, to be told they are all one in Christ may be puzzling or even upsetting. I hope to help the children see that they are all of value in God's eyes, that even their individual differences are of value.

# MATERIALS

No new materials will be needed for the cafeteria activities or the paper theater and tags begun yesterday.

I have a copy of *The Whole World Singing*, so we can try some of the action songs if the group is in a singing mood.

The Biggle-Gog story (page 49 in the junior textbook) seems to be just what we need now. I have my props left over from the last time I taught this course.

# CHECK OF TEXTBOOK SUGGESTIONS

Our children, having already made name cards for themselves, will need little or no explanation about how to make name cards for the Biggles and Bogs and the Siggles and Sogs for dramatizing the story. (Check page 50 for card colors, pages 52, 53 for names.) I shall do as suggested and make a mystery of the cards, telling the children that when they are finished I'll let them know what it is all about. We shall act out the story as I read it.

# SCHEDULE

**Cafeteria activities (8:45-9:30):** Only a few children will actually need these today. Try to involve Calo and Alex in some satisfying activity. Avoid saying *no* and *don't* as much as possible. Try to keep to positive invitations.

Enlist the help of all children who are willing so that the mysterious card-making operation can be finished before 9:30. While this work is going on the teachers can lead the conversation to ways in which people differ — physical differences, color, names, where they live, abilities, and the like.

About 9:30 I shall read the Biggle-Gog story, using the suggestions for dramatization on pages 53-56. I think I know the children well enough now (and they know me) so that we can work together on this, but we shall see.

**Transition (10:15-10:30):** Snack time and recess (Instead of the usual games we might try the suggestion on page 59 in the junior textbook to sing and act out songs from *The Whole World Singing*. Or we may do this for a break between the two parts of the story if the dramatization goes slowly.)

**Group time (10:30-11:15):** Read and discuss the Bible passages that are appropriate. Some of the ideas and the questions on pages 58 and 59 of the junior textbook might help our group to think through these verses. Relate Psalm 145:9 and Acts 17:24-27 to the earlier discussion of early man and how his differences gradually developed. If the group is still with me we can read Colossians 3:11 or Galatians 3:28 and translate it freely to help the children understand that even though we are all different we are united through the love of Jesus Christ.

If the children get more than fun out of the Biggle-Gog story, we may be able to have an enriching Bible study. Otherwise we shall take one of the selections and try to put it into our own words to be used in worship.

During this time some children will return to active work. They may want to make a paper theater of the Biggle-Gog story, drawing stick figures. They can use colored crayons to make the blonde and black hair, white chalk for the pale-skinned people. Black and white stick figures would be best for the second part of the story to show, for instance, the different ways of saying " hello " with body antics.

Some children may want to bring this story up to date by discussing the possibility of God's having created people on other planets. This may lead to making a papier-mâché solar system (see page 114 Resource Section in this book).

**Worship (11:15-11:45):** Plan the worship with a small committee. Other activities will continue as during the last period. Perhaps we shall continue the thinking of yesterday's meditation that in a world full of individual differences all can perform friendly acts. This small group might like to learn a hymn, such as " Maker of the Planets " (No. 6 in *Hymns for Junior Worship*). Possible

Bible readings are the suggested verses from the Book of Psalms or the selection from Acts 17.

# THURSDAY NIGHT

I might have known it would take an earthquake to involve Calo and Alex! While the children were making the cards under the direction of Maria and Rosa, I took Calo and Alex aside and with a great show of secrecy showed them the props for dramatizing the Biggle-Gog story. Being sound men for an earthquake scene struck them as the supreme opportunity. Lesser channels could never provide an outlet for their vim and vigor! I wondered if their interest would end with the earthquake, but they looked upon the whole dramatization as a television presentation and stayed with me to the end, moving the props with real enjoyment and acting out parts with a skill that brought spontaneous applause from the children several times. There was some horseplay, of course, but not so much that we couldn't control it. The Biggle-Gog story is *made* for juniors — even for inner-city juniors.

Our problems with these two boys are not yet solved, but at least they now have had one experience of feeling themselves part of the group. I believe we should do more dramatizing next week. Why not the story of Zacchaeus as it is told in the junior pupil's book?

# FRIDAY

# we're all alike

*(Adaptation of Session 5, Junior Textbook)*

With two fairly successful sessions behind us I think that tomorrow we shall be able to follow the basic suggestions for Session 5 in the junior textbook except for dramatizing the various December festivals. We still need to develop more appreciation for one another before attempting to highlight the richness of differences.

## PURPOSE

With our inner-city children we shall not go further into how and why people differ or the values and reasons for these differences as suggested in the textbook statement of purpose. *Our purpose in this session will be to help the children realize how many things people have in common.*

## BIBLE

The children may not realize that one of the things people have in common is the longing to know God and his will. I shall tell briefly the mysterious story of Job and read Job 23:3 and Psalm 42:1-2. Perhaps the latter verses will inspire the children to illustrate them. These inner-city children may not know what a deer or a hart is, but they can understand thirst and how a swiftly running animal might pant for water. They may understand too the wistfulness of the rich young ruler in Luke 18:18-23 who longed to know God, but could not bring himself to pay the price.

40

We can use the story of Philip and the Ethiopian from Acts 8: 26-38 as it is retold in the junior textbook (page 75) to help our pupils understand that Christianity is one link between many different people.

# MATERIALS

I shall take my copy of *The Family of Man* to church and use it to stimulate discussion for the poster-making project suggested on pages 64-66 in the junior textbook, " All People Everywhere Like to. . . ." I believe I have enough copies of *Life* magazine to take, too, so that the children will have pictures to cut out for illustrating the posters. We have enough poster board for as many posters as they may want to make.

The story of Philip and the Ethiopian in the junior textbook does not lend itself to dramatization, but a tableau might be worked out. I'll take the box of scarves and draperies we use for dramatizing Bible stories in my own church school. The chariot could be painted with easel paints, but I'll have to look up a larger brush or two. I have a bright-colored picture of Philip and the Ethiopian showing a magnificent, jeweled chariot. That should impress the two boys and indeed all these children who seem to love splendor and color and lavishness of any kind. We could make an effective, colorful scene, pose it with real children, and let the other children look at it while I read the story.

I'll want a copy of *The Whole World Singing* to use again after the snacks. The group seemed to enjoy acting out the songs this morning.

# CHECK OF TEXTBOOK SUGGESTIONS

In addition to looking up magazines to take from home I might find in the church some old church school material with pictures that could be cut out to use on the posters. I like the idea of illustrating the posters with Bible people as well as people of today. Emphasizing ways in which people of Bible times were like people today may help these boys and girls realize that the Bible is the story of real people who were learning to know God.

The idea of making a " New Words and Names I Have Learned " booklet has not seemed to fit in with the needs and interests of this inner-city group. One or two of the children might have enjoyed doing it as an individual project if I had had time to help them with planning and developing it.

Omit the dramatization of various festivals.

# SCHEDULE

**Cafeteria activities (8:45):** Available as usual, but many children may want to work immediately on unfinished projects to make them ready for the party for the parents tonight. Perhaps Calo and Alex could be challenged to make a chariot with cardboard boxes for the tableau.

As the children work at the various activities we'll begin conversations about likenesses as suggested on page 64 in the junior textbook. The magazines will be there and large sheets of poster board with headings printed as suggested on pages 65, 66. Each group might choose one or two of the headings and work independently to illustrate the posters, sharing their efforts at worship time.

**Transition (10:00):** We'll sing and act out the songs from *The Whole World Singing* that we tried yesterday (junior textbook, page 59). As the customs of the countries are acted out we'll try to think of similar or related customs in American life today. Then we'll serve the snack.

**Group time (10:15):** After the snack we shall talk about the fact that all people everywhere long to know God and his will (unless this fact has come up earlier in the discussions). I can tell the stories of Job and the rich young ruler briefly. If I present Psalm 42:1-2 with pictures of deer, perhaps some children will want to illustrate it.

**10:45-11:15:** Prepare for the open house party tonight. Be sure all the children have received enough tickets to give to their parents and friends, brothers and sisters. Tidy up the room, but leave the easels, the clay, and other evidences of what the children have been doing. Tell the children to invite their parents to sit down at the clay table with them, paint a picture, or try their hand at some of the other work.

Be sure all displays of the children's work, such as paper theaters, clay figures, or paintings have attached to them cards with a word of explanation about their meaning and purpose. Two easel pictures may be displayed together with a card saying, "After Joe painted this (scribbled, muddy mess), he painted this (picture of the boys and girls listening to a story as seen from the rear)." Clay modeling might need a word of explanation too, such as, "Cats and dogs fight like this (clay dog chasing a clay cat), but people can talk things out (clay people sitting in a circle)."

**11:15:** As the worship is being planned for this morning, the committee may want to think about making the service suitable for use this evening too. If a chariot has been made and a tableau arranged, one child might read the story of Philip and the Ethiopian as it appears in the junior textbook (page 75). In addition to the preparatory remarks that are given in the textbook, the reader (or some other child) may want to say that the children have discovered many different things that people everywhere have in common, and among them is the longing to know God and his will. The children may not know the hymn, "Man's Unceasing Quest for God" (No. 67 in *Hymns for Junior Worship*), but the parents may be able to help them sing it tonight. The words of "Manitou Listens to Me" (No. 116 in *The Whole World Singing*) may be used as a prayer.

# OPEN HOUSE

**Saturday morning:** I can't believe I have known these children only five days! I realize I have spent more time thinking about them and planning for them than I spend with groups at home. But still it has been only five days! And last night I felt their feelings!

I glowed with the same pride and importance they showed as they ushered in their parents, relatives, and friends. One girl brought the lady next door because her mother was sick. "She can tell my mother about it," said the child. "My mother likes to talk to her better than she likes to listen to me."

Calo and Alex came with their respective big sisters who, like the boys, seem to be enemy-friends. Calo said without the least embarrassment, "My ma won't come. She won't go anywhere where his ma is going." And Alex said, "Mine either."

The sisters are only a bit older than the girls in our senior group. I invited them to join us next week, but they both work at the ten-cent store. They were frankly curious about what had been going on here, but refused to try out the clay work and painting as the other adults were doing. Instead, they followed the boys around, chattering to each other and punctuating their chatter with sharp commands evidently meant to keep the boys in line. Their scolding words were hurled at the boys with no relationship to the behavior of the moment. When Calo was standing perfectly still, absorbed in watching a grandfather paint, his sister said sharply, "Get along there!" But when Alex was about to put a dripping paint brush into the coat pocket of an adult guest, the girls were looking the other way and I had to be the one to stop him. A minute afterwards when the boys were in no trouble at all, they were both ordered to "Come here and shut up!" The boys paid absolutely no attention to their sisters' commands. The sisters didn't seem to expect them to.

In a sense this whole neighborhood seems to live and act in this cut-and-dried manner. They speak their lines, they do this and that; but there is no relation between what they do and their real desires, needs and yearnings. There is no purpose to what they do. They do not seem to have hopes of accomplishing any purpose.

I began to see why Calo and Alex didn't seem to hear me either. I listened carefully to the girls' voices and way of speaking so that next week I will be able to pitch and phrase my requests in an entirely different — and I hope — ear-opening manner.

The boys did not do too much damage. They knocked down some displays, slammed some doors, punched at each other now and then. But they carried cups of juice to their sisters and helped mop up some paint that was spilled by an adult guest. They knew where the big mops were kept and tore down the hall after them before I had time to ask them to help.

The other children were shiny-eyed and excited. All of them were on their best behavior. Some of the guests were reluctant to try their hand at the " kid stuff," but the children cajoled them into it. The evening session buzzed with the same work-talk sounds that we had been hearing every morning.

Marc and I wished we could have let the " free time " go on and on so that we might have had more and longer talks with more of the adults. Marc said he seldom gets to speak to his parishioners in such a congenial atmosphere. " In their homes, and when I see them one by one on the street," he said, " they are always so guarded." After last night's conversations we are confidently expecting to see several of them at Sunday services and perhaps some of the men at the Workshop Night Marc holds once a month.

We didn't come together for refreshments, but let the children offer juice and cookies to their parents whenever the time seemed right for it. Marc and I could continue our conversation with one group while we suggested that the child and his guest, who had just finished working at the clay table, wash up and help themselves to refreshments.

Rosa and Maria, however, knowing I had planned a worship period, began directing people to the gathering place in the alcove after the work-talk period had gone on for about an hour. The girl who had planned to read the story of Philip and the Ethiopian came to me with a white face and whispered, " Please, do I have to read? " I turned to Marc who offered to do it if she would walk around quietly and show everyone the picture while he read.

This was an excellent alternative to what might have been a strained performance. In planning a guest night or party, I had tried to keep the program as much like our daily sessions as possible, but I suppose it takes more than a week for them to free themselves from their restraints.

How strange this is. They have restraints which keep them from functioning freely as contributing members of a learning group, yet in other areas I have been struggling all week to help these children develop some self-restraint!

Before Marc read, I welcomed everyone more formally and spoke of the warm feeling of fellowship that had been prevalent all evening. I led the group in a brief prayer of thanks for this friendliness and a petition that it would spread itself through the church and the neighborhood.

Then I told how the children had been discovering many different things people everywhere have in common. The children joined in with a few comments when I questioned them. I led into the story by telling how we had begun to realize this morning that everywhere everyone secretly or openly seems to have the longing to know God and his will even as the Ethiopian did.

I realized that even with the guitar we might not be able to struggle through the hymn " Man's Unceasing Quest for God " since we did not have a hymn-singing congregation. I asked Rosa's cousin to strum the guitar softly while I read the words and told them it was a favorite hymn of the boys and girls I taught in the church in my community.

After this we all sang together. Some of the parents, too, knew " He's Got the Whole World in His Hands."

Marc then led us in the Lord's prayer. At the door, after the benediction, he shook hands and invited everyone to come Sunday to find God together.

This week has been a good preparation for another deeper and more purposeful and organized week of work and play and worship together. I feel this is some of the most rewarding and purposeful work I have ever done, and I thank God for this opportunity.

# SECTION 2 | plans for primaries

# PRIMARY CHILDREN
# AND THEIR NEEDS

**What they are like:** All kinds of studies have been made to help us understand ages and stages of child development. We know that most six-, seven-, and eight-year-olds are charged with energy (although they need frequent rest to recharge their batteries) and are constantly active in every sense of the word. A six-year-old does not sit *still* to listen to a story. He taps his feet, moves his hands and fingers, wriggles or nods almost every minute. Primary children are eager learners rapidly working towards self-sufficiency and more independence.

At the beginning of this age span you can't expect too much co-operation from the child. His desires for self-sufficiency and independence far outreach his abilities so he is often in a state of rebellion or confusion. He doesn't seem to like himself or anyone else. He strives to produce for his own glory. He wants to be right all the time, to win every game.

He works hard at learning skills — throwing balls, jumping rope, spinning Yo-yos. If his muscles and nervous system are developing at a good rate he can achieve enough to satisfy himself and gain a feeling of self-respect. If development is slower than his desire to do, there is trouble and he sometimes gets violently emotional.

In spite of these problems he endears himself to teachers with his eagerness to learn, his curiosity and imagination, and his infectious laughter.

By age seven there is a leveling off and the average child is striving more to do things well rather than just to do things. He becomes less aggravating (except that he may be as slow as a snail because of his tendency to dreaminess) but remains worried and concerned about himself and how others treat him. He needs to feel important, somehow. He may begin collecting. At this age an assortment of picture cards becomes precious. If he has the opportunity, he will collect snakes, worms, and beetles too. He tries very hard to be known for something or to be good at something. He wants to make a name for himself.

Seven-year-olds are beginning to relate more to other children. This is a period of best friends, but it is also the time of " proving " oneself to the peer group. For boys this often means developing prowess in wrestling. For girls it may be ability to turn handsprings or fancy rope-jumping or it may be bragging about possessions — dolls, clothes, jewelry, or collections.

When he does finally gain status in the eyes of other children — about the time he is eight — he gives his whole loyalty to a group of his peers. If you can fit in with the laws they agree upon among themselves you will be obeyed; otherwise, perhaps not. On the other hand, throughout these primary years the child has been developing a sense of right and wrong, and by age eight a sense of fairness may appear. Sometimes this leads to tattling, other times it actually leads to the ability to accept reprimands or censure for not playing fair. There is a surface rebellion against the reprimand, but inside the child knows he deserves it and may even be glad for punishment that eases his sense of guilt.

Because of environmental problems inner-city primary children may be more worldly-wise but less intellectually advanced than other children in their age group. They have a much better understanding of the values and use of money, for instance, than most suburban children, but knowledge of elementary science may be much less.

**Meeting their needs:** Any program we plan for six- to eight-year-olds must take into account the needs for activity, achievement in skills leading to independence, and the developing relationships between the children. We also have to think about their deeper needs: the need to develop a sense of trust through experiences with trustworthy adults who help them know the trustworthiness of God; the need to be loved so that they may come to know God's love and reach out to others with love; the need to know themselves as persons of worth, created in the image of God, so that they can respect themselves and others.

The vacation church school course *Friends From Many Lands* can be adapted to help meet the special needs of inner-city children in all the above areas and also open doors to becoming friends with children of many races and nationalities and to the realization that all children are children of God.

**Equipment and materials:** You will want to have paint, easels, crayons, large sheets of paper, paste, scissors, odds and ends for making collages, and clay for your cafeteria activities. (If you are a primary teacher and have opened the book to this section to begin your reading, you will want to turn back to Section 1 to read about the cafeteria approach and teaching in a ministering context – also the advice from experienced teachers.) A large boxful of assorted buttons will be used imaginatively by the children.

If you have space — in your room, in the hall, in an outdoor area — have several rubber balls for playing catch, one or two long jump ropes and some short ones, perhaps even an old mattress for tumbling.

Many inner-city children have never had blocks for building. If blocks of assorted sizes and shapes are not available, usable ones can be made by taping shut sturdy boxes and cartons. Coats of paint and shellac add both durability and attractiveness. Lumber dealers often have odds and ends of wood available at a minimal cost. Sanding and shellacking the pieces can be one of the cafeteria activities. Toy cars, trucks and planes will increase the possibilities of the block center.

Again if you have space, set up a housekeeping corner as one of your cafeteria activities. A tea table, small chairs (these have a special fascination for children who do not have them in their homes – even a gangling eight-year-old will fold himself into one of these chairs and pretend to be a father), a doll bed and a cupboard (may be two boxes set one on top of the other) are the essential furnishings. Dolls, dishes, doll blankets and other items should be clean and attractive. If the church does not have a tea table or doll bed, these can usually be obtained at small cost from Goodwill Industries. Chairs can be borrowed from the nursery or kindergarten.

Growing plants and pictures add to the attractiveness of the room. A globe is an item of special interest to primaries and would be useful with this course. A book corner with a few easy-to-read books, picture-storybooks of children at work and play, and nature or science books will encourage boys and girls to avail themselves of the wonderful world of books. The primary textbook suggests a number of books related to the course.

You may not be able to have all the equipment and materials suggested but try to have a big enough variety to meet the needs and interests of all your pupils.

**Caring for equipment and materials:** Although children in this age group are developing a sense of right and wrong, they are still rather vague about *mine* and *thine*. They may pocket things that they like to play with–whether it be buttons, crayons, a lump of clay, or a toy car. This is not stealing in the usual sense of the word. In the more deprived areas of the inner city, however, children at a very young age are often taught the art of stealing.

We can help our vacation church school pupils by keeping tempting items put away except when they are in use. At the end of the cafeteria period you might have two older children be the garage and hangar attendants to collect the toy cars, trucks and planes from the block corner and put them in a box or on a shelf in the cupboard. "House mothers" might be assigned to put the dolls to bed and stack the dishes in the cupboard. A "keeper of the clay" and a "collector of crayons" could be responsible for collecting these items and putting them in the proper containers. These should be readily available for restless children to use under the supervision of one of the teachers or helpers during the latter part of the session. A "librarian" may check to see that all the books are on the shelf or stacked neatly on the table. If the children help with these responsibilities, they will be achieving a sense of trustworthiness and ability as well as being taught respect for property and ownership.

# PRIMARY SESSION PLANS

The following five session plans are adapted from Plans 1, 3, 4, 9, and 10 of the primary textbook. In a ten-day vacation church school, the first two sessions can be expanded to three sessions by using additional materials from the textbook and from General Plan 3 in this book. Session 4 in these plans may be rescheduled as the last session of the second week using additional suggestions from the textbook if a closing program is planned.

You will want to read all of the primary textbook and check the stories, activities, songs, and other materials that you think may be useful with your pupils. Read especially the "To Think About" sections in the session plans and the biblical passages suggested for your meditation as you prepare for each day's task. These will help you to minister to the children in the name and company of Jesus.

# SESSION 1

# friendliness

*(Adaptation of Plan 1, Primary Textbook)*

## PURPOSE

The purpose suggested in the primary textbook for the first session is "to help the children think of the members of their group as friends." This is not quite so easy to work at in the inner city as it is in areas where children are less ready to fight at the drop of a hat. It is unwise to expect inner-city children to do much thinking and discussing the first day they are together in a new group.

It would be more prudent to arrange a welcoming, friendly room and prepare a wealth of inviting activities that will catch and absorb their interest. Inner-city children need many ways in which to express their thoughts and feelings besides in words. *A more effective purpose for you to work on may be to give the children an experience of being befriended.* Discovering that the other members of the group – at least some of them – are their friends may be a by-product or bonus!

## MATERIALS

Cafeteria activities (see Section 1 and Resource Section of this book) should be laid out for primary children just as for juniors. Painting, clay work, blocks and toys, housekeeping equipment, pictures to talk about with an adult, books to browse in, bright paper to cut and paste, material for name tags — all this work should be ready to jump into when the first child arrives.

# BIBLE

The experienced teachers, you will recall, advised us not to rush into Bible study with inner-city children. A great many of them do not have enough religious training and background to make Bible study meaningful. This is even more true of primaries than of juniors. We can communicate the Bible story of God's redemptive love through relationships with the children in which we express to them love, forgiveness, justice, and mercy on the human level. Thus we may become channels of God's love.

Four Bible passages are suggested for possible use in the first plan in the primary textbook: Proverbs 18:24; 27:10; 17:17, and John 15:12-17. Proverbs 17:17a is appropriate to use in the worship service. In the informal conversation during the cafeteria activities or snack time you might use Proverbs 18:24. Proverbs 27:10 is difficult and probably will not have much meaning for inner-city primaries. The passage from John should be in your mind and freely translated in your own words if an appropriate moment arrives. Beware of saying, " Jesus tells us that we should love one another as he loves us." Children who are not familiar with the stories of Jesus may think that he is a person living today who is giving them orders.

# SCHEDULE

**Cafeteria activities:** Have every child make a name tag. These may be smiling faces as suggested in the primary textbook. Let each child draw a happy face on a sheet of construction paper and print his name above or below the face. (You may have to do the printing for some of the children.) If you don't know your pupils at all you may want them " labeled " front and back, sandwich-board style. The back name tag might have a funny face or a drawing of the child's hand. Fasten both cards to over-the-shoulder straps or strings and tie the sides together at the waist (so the name tags will not interfere with children's activities.)

During the cafeteria period some children may want to play the game, " Naming Friends," or " Punchinello," as suggested in the primary textbook. Do not feel hurt if your smiling invitation draws no response but stares. One of the suggested filmstrips (see the primary textbook) may arouse more interest, but children who are used to fast-moving television westerns do not always sit still for filmstrips either. An expectant attitude, however, on the part of the teacher sometimes calls forth attention. The thing to avoid is the moment of boredom that comes when the projector doesn't work and the lights are already out. It might take you all morning to recover from the pandemonium let loose.

It is far better to allow a long period of free activity with a friendly adult at each interest center to deal with disorder or disinterest the moment it breaks out. Conversation about who our friends are can go on in every group, the leader making notes of interesting contributions that might be shared with the whole group later and perhaps be made the nucleus of a filmstrip (see Plan 1 in primary textbook) or one of the projects suggested under the heading "Ideas in Concrete Form," page 111 of this book.

If you assure the children that the paint, the paper, the clay are for them to use, after a first shy moment (you may have to move away) the children will be busy. Those not interested in paint or clay can make name tags, build with blocks, play in the housekeeping corner, or look at pictures with a teacher.

**Transition:** After an hour or more of such activity there should be some sort of a break, even if the children seem absorbed in the activities. Without ringing a bell or expecting everyone to drop what he is doing at once, perhaps you can begin to gather some of the children into a group.

You might walk around with a banjo or a guitar, singing a folk song or "Friends, Friends, Friends." The words and music for the latter are in the primary textbook. You might sit down next to a record player and put on a record of folk songs. If the children don't know how to sing them, they can clap to the rhythm. Or you might collect some of the paintings and ask the owners if you may show them to the other boys and girls.

Children are usually willing and interested to move in and see what two or three other children and a teacher are looking at or doing. They flock together as a crowd gathers on a street corner. Those who do object mightily to joining the group can be calmly assured that they may go on with their work if they would rather stay by themselves than be with the others. If four or five stay in an interest center, a teacher should stay with them to help them remember that they must be as quiet as possible while the other children are trying to sing and listen.

You can't expect to have any work center cleaned up neat as a pin on the first day. Leave materials available, anyway, because many children may want to return to them after group and snack time. The second session will be soon enough to appoint helpers to take specific responsibilities.

If the group is large it will be well during story or discussion or worship time to have an extra adult on hand who can accompany an acting-up child on an errand outside the room. The errand may be to the kitchen to get the cartons of milk and a basket of graham crackers for snack time.

Between songs the story teacher may send children out in groups of three or four to go to the bathroom and wash their hands. Just before snack time the children do not care to wander too far afield, but especially on the first day the teachers should keep each child in the circle of their awareness. A complete dismissal for the group might mean great difficulty in getting them together again after recess.

**Group time:** This could begin with the snack. You might sing these words as an up-and-down-the-scale grace: "Thank you for the friends we meet; and thank you for the food we eat." (See page 107.)

While the children are eating, you might tell an adapted version of the story about Peter, the migrant boy who felt accepted after he had played his harmonica for the group (primary textbook, Plan 1). Can you make it interesting to your particular children? In adapting the story think: What might a child of this group share as a surprise with other children? A trick with a Yo-yo? A whistled tune? A pet parrot? Write the story down the way you tell it this time because it may be used again, or at least referred to, in a later session.

If the story does not seem adaptable to your group, you might use "Limp the Chimp" in the story section of this book. Afterwards ask the children if they can discover in themselves some friendship-making "muscles" they didn't know they had.

Share the pictures and any work done this morning that the children care to describe. Share the high points of the conversations about friends that occurred earlier in the interest centers. Invite the children to bring things to show – the more we know about each other, the better we understand each other. Understanding leads to friendship.

Sing "Friends, Friends, Friends" and also introduce the song "God Is the Loving Father" (No. 37, *Hymns for Primary Worship*). Song charts will help the children learn the words.

**Worship:** Show a Bible and make introductory remarks if necessary. You might consider the worship suggestions in General Plan 1 in this book. Perhaps tell the story "Jesus and the Bible" (page 93). Use the silent and spoken prayers suggested in the primary textbook, Plan 1, or phrase your own prayer of thanks for friends and friendly acts. Read Proverbs 17: 17a or have a child read it.

**Activities:** If there is time afterwards the books of friends or other friendship projects, such as the friendship kerchief described in the Resource Section of this book, may be worked on by those who are interested. Other children should go back to the unfinished work of the morning. If the primary Activity Sheet No. 1 is available you may give it to the children at the end of the morning. Ask them to fill it out and get individual expressions of how the vacation church school looked and felt to each child. These insights will help in your later plans.

You may want to introduce the friendship circle and the friendship song to the group the first day. The song and description of the circle are on page 107 of this book.

# SESSION 2

# friendliness in our neighborhood

*(Adaptation of Plan 3, Primary Textbook)*

If you are not well acquainted with the families of your pupils and their school situations you may not wish to use Plan 2, " Friends at Home and School," in the primary textbook. For a ten-day vacation church school you could develop an extra session from the suggestions in Plans 1 and 3 in the primary textbook and General Plan 3 in this book.

## PURPOSE

A multiple purpose is given for this session in the primary textbook. It may be kept in mind by inner-city teachers if you will not feel anxious because you cannot begin to accomplish all of it in one morning, or even in one week.

In the first session the children had an experience of being able to give and receive friendliness in the church, which is part of their community. In this session the children might evaluate their community as a whole. Is it a place where friendliness is given and received? If not, what can be done about it? *The purpose for the inner-city boys and girls may be to look for and contribute to expressions of friendliness in the community.*

58

# MATERIALS

Continue to provide the equipment and materials for cafeteria activities introduced in the first session. Have materials available for friendship projects begun yesterday or to be started today. If you have the Activity Sheets that accompany the primary textbook, Sheet No. 4 may be used in this session.

# BIBLE

The story of Ruth, suggested for use with Plan 3 in the primary textbook, may have little meaning for inner-city primaries who know nothing about how grain grows in a field and for whom "long ago in a faraway land" can mean when their parents were young and lived in another part of the city or another country.

Matthew 22:39 will have meaning for the children in the light of their experiences in the first session and in this session. Ephesians 4:32 and Hebrews 13:2a have difficult words and some concepts that will be unfamiliar to your pupils.

# SCHEDULE

**Cafeteria activities:** The room should be set up again with cafeteria activities in abundance. You may get the group together for conversation about the community very early in the morning as the primary textbook suggests. Or you may not! The suggested songs, "Friends, Friends, Friends" and "I Love My Friends and They Love Me," can be sung informally while the children are working in the various interest centers as well as when they are sitting in a circle.

Work can gradually change from the aggression-relieving stage to the purposeful stage as the teachers at the clay table, the painting area, the paper cutting and pasting area, the block corner and the housekeeping corner ask such questions as: Did you ever see the inside of that big church that is two blocks down the street? Is there a ten-cent store in the neighborhood? Are there any empty lots? What does your house look like? Your school?

Gradually parts of the community can be represented in some of the materials. Eventually these representations could be put together to make a mural, a table-top panorama, or a three-dimensional scene as suggested in the primary textbook and page 115 of the Resource Section of this book. Activity Sheet No. 4 may be used to provide cutout figures of community workers in the murals or the three-dimensional scenes.

When the children gather around their project either to work on it or to admire it, you may introduce the suggestions in the primary textbook, Plan 3, about community conversations and the guessing game to help the children think about people who work for them.

**Transition:** The song "Friends, Friends, Friends" may be appropriate following this conversation and game. Sing one or two songs the children know, perhaps practice "God Is the Loving Father" (No. 37, *Hymns for Primary Worship*) and the friendship song (page 107, this book). Play a circle game such as "Looby Loo" or one of the games suggested in the primary textbook. During the singing you can again excuse a few children at a time to wash up and get ready for the snack.

**Group time:** Inner-city children can investigate the friendliness and helpfulness of the community by going out in pairs to various stores to ask for contributions of cardboard boxes for the vacation church school program. Before they leave discuss and role-play friendly ways of making the request. Talk about the importance of not disturbing the store people when they are busy with customers. Suggest that the children pretend to be storekeepers and then let them say how they wish children would act when they come into the store (not touch food or merchandise until they have purchased it, not be rowdy or noisy, not run between the shelves and play).

You may feel that your children are not yet enough of a group to leave the classroom to carry out this project. You might follow the suggestions for the discussion and role-playing and have the children pair off to gather boxes during the afternoon. When they bring the boxes in the next morning they can tell about their experiences and make plans as suggested below. This would give more time in this session for the children to use cafeteria activities and to work on the friendship projects.

The children may come back and report on friendliness or unfriendliness they have discovered. This may lead to a discussion about what the boys and girls can do to express friendliness in a special way to the entire community.

Is there an empty lot full of rubbish that could be cleaned out and planted with grass or flowers to make an oasis in the concrete and asphalt? Is there a family with someone ill who might like the children to take turns going to the store for them? Is there a cross old man who has been annoyed by the noise children make around his house? Could he be changed to a friendly person if two or three of the children would go to see him and tell him they have just realized that noise gives him a headache and they will play on the other side of the street after this?

Guidance in thinking about people of other religions, races, or culture groups may be postponed until the next week, but a letter of welcome can be sent, as suggested in the primary textbook, to any newcomers in the neighborhood. Invite the children to come to vacation church school too.

Books of friends or any other friendship project begun yesterday may be worked on. Little paper flags can be placed over pictures of buildings or places in the community scene where friendliness occurred today. This could be a continuing operation throughout the course.

The first chapter of the primary pupil's book might be read to the children. Or the story in this book, " When the Other Side Came Over," (page 103) might be used.

**Worship:** This may begin with the song " Friends, Friends, Friends." The children might compose a litany, each child telling of some instance of friendliness and the other children responding by saying together: " We are always glad about friendliness, God. Help us to feel friendly toward others."

Close by singing " God Is the Loving Father " and make a friendship circle for singing the friendship song.

General Plan 3 in this book suggests further ideas that may be used in this session.

# SESSION 3

# friends we do not see

*(Adaptation of Plan 4, Primary Textbook)*

## PURPOSE

Part of the purpose suggested in the primary textbook for this session may be used for an inner-city plan. It may be stated in this way: *To help the children realize that friends are not always the persons they often see, to help them appreciate the persons in many lands whose work provides some of the food we eat and other products we use, to help them begin to think about the fact that God is the loving father of children everywhere.*

## MATERIALS

You may want to have a display of objects showing how people keep in touch with faraway friends. Activity Sheet No. 5 may be used to inspire the children to set up a place of beauty in the classroom.

## BIBLE

Use Psalm 75: 1a as the call to worship as suggested in the primary textbook. The other passages listed, Proverbs 20: 11, Malachi 2: 10a, b, and Romans 12: 9-18, may be used if they fit in with the conversation at any time. The verse from Proverbs might be threatening to some children. The passage from Romans will have to be translated into simpler language, but after the children understand the meaning, verses 9 and 10 might be read directly from the Bible.

# SCHEDULE

**Cafeteria activities:** Allow plenty of time for the children to have satisfying turns with two or more of the activities provided. If some of the boys and girls are aimlessly drifting from one center to another, call their attention to the display of objects showing how people keep in touch with friends far away. Gradually you may guide the other pupils to the display. Or you may simply ask questions about how people keep in touch, as the children continue painting, modeling, cutting, and pasting. They may be inspired to use the materials to represent planes, trains, greeting cards, telephones, boats, or automobiles. Actual greeting cards may be painted, or cut and pasted, and used.

When modeled or pictured planes, trains, ships, and such are finished, they may be grouped and displayed with an explanatory card. Other work that has been done by the children thus far should also be grouped and displayed with explanatory cards written by the teachers.

**Transition:** Gather the group together for songs and games, washing hands, and the snack.

**Group time:** Call attention to the display of work the children have completed. When they see what they have done so far they may be receptive to the idea of a party for their parents. In inner-city programs a party at the end of the first week will give occasion for the parents and teachers to meet and so help the teachers know the children more thoroughly while they are still working with them. A simple open house program may be planned. The time must be decided upon, and tickets or invitations should be made and taken home by the children today.

If there is time the Activity Sheet No. 5 may inspire the children to make a place of beauty in their vacation church school room to use as a worship center. Help them obtain the best effect possible from available materials and furniture. Perhaps a local florist would lend a few potted plants, at least for the evening of the party for the parents.

At story time, if the story of Marjorie in Plan 4 of the primary textbook is used, samples of rice, cotton cloth, sugar, cocoa should be passed around for the children to see, touch, and taste — if they like. The pictures and reading cards you may have prepared according to the suggestions in the textbook will help the children know their world friends and the work they do. These may be examined at this time too.

**Worship:** The worship plans for this session may be used exactly as described in the primary textbook. The worship might be more meaningful if the discussion of the second chapter in the primary pupil's book could directly precede worship.

At the close of the session make a friendship circle and sing the friendship song.

# SESSION 4

# something in common

*(Adaptation of Plan 9, Primary Textbook)*

## PURPOSE

The purpose of this session as stated in the primary textbook is appropriate for inner-city children. We too want *to help our children to think about the friends they have met either directly or vicariously and to grow in their understanding that children everywhere are alike in important ways, such as feelings and needs.*

At the time of this session the inner-city children may not have had the wide acquaintance with children of the world that other children have had before the ninth session in the primary textbook, but the story of Marjorie, and the reading cards used yesterday should have given the boys and girls some feeling of the world beyond their neighborhood. Also they have friends in the group and friends in the community to consider for likenesses.

## MATERIALS

No new materials except Activity Sheet No. 10 will be needed for today. Check your picture display and other displays around the room to be sure that there are a number of things that will stimulate

65

children's thinking about likenesses when they take the quiet walk around the room as suggested in the primary textbook.

# BIBLE

Whether or not you have used Malachi 2:10a, b, previously, this can be used in this session. 1 Corinthians 12:4-14 should be put into words the children can understand.

# SCHEDULE

**Cafeteria activities:** The quiet walk around the room to look at pictures and other displays for the purpose of discovering ways in which children everywhere are alike can be taken by the children one by one as the others are at work finishing projects for the displays. They may need the personal attention of a teacher as they take the walk if they are going to understand what they are to do. Instead of asking the boys and girls to write their ideas — if writing or making these comparisons is difficult for your pupils — those who have ideas may whisper them to a teacher who can write them on slips of paper for each of the children to put in the box.

Some children, of course, should be allowed to paint for the sheer joy of painting instead of doing a project.

**Transition:** Follow your usual procedure of singing, dismissing a few children at a time to wash their hands, play games, and have the snack. Your choice of games will depend upon the cafeteria activities chosen. If most of the boys and girls chose art activities, use a running game or some other active game that will give their muscles a chance to stretch. If they need a chance to relax, a quiet game such as " Button, Button, Who's Got the Button? " would be more appropriate. (It is hard for primaries to wait for turns. For a game such as " Button, Button " divide into small circles of five or six each.)

**Group time:** Begin group time by opening the box with the slips of paper telling ways in which children everywhere are alike. Make a list of these as suggested in the primary textbook.

You may use the story of Peter again to stimulate more thoughts about universal feelings and needs and likes. Be sure you tell the story exactly as you adapted it in Session 1.

Activity Sheet No. 10 will stimulate thinking along these lines too.

Develop the choral reading according to the suggestions in Plan 9 of the primary textbook. If this seems too great an undertaking for your group, print the heading "All Children Everywhere" on a large sheet of poster board, print the lists of likenesses underneath, and let the children find magazine pictures to cut out and paste on for illustrations. If you do not have magazines, the children may crayon pictures of children singing, playing games, enjoying pets, sleeping, eating, and the like.

Sometime during the morning sing the song "God Is the Loving Father," so that the children will know it well when the parents come. Practice saying Malachi 2:10a together too so that it may be used in the evening worship if the children have not created a choral reading.

**Worship:** This song, this Bible verse, and a brief prayer of thankfulness to God for his love and care that extend to children everywhere may be the nucleus of the worship this morning too.

Don't forget to make a friendship circle and sing the friendship song before the children leave.

# SESSION 5

# god loves us all

*(Adaptation of Plan 10, Primary Textbook)*

## PURPOSE

The purpose as stated in Plan 10 of the primary textbook is an excellent one for the fifth session in this series: " *To help the children realize that children everywhere are children of one Father, God, and that he loves them all; to help them realize they can help others to know about God's love; to share with parents and friends their experiences and learning during the study.*"

## MATERIALS

Same as in previous sessions. Have song chart " God Is the Loving Father " ready for the children to illustrate. Activity Sheet No. 11 may be used. If you plan to have the children collect bugs, get some glass containers and a supply of rubber bands to fasten perforated transparent paper over the tops if needed.

## BIBLE

Malachi 2:10a, b, will be used again. The reference in 1 Corinthians 3:7-10 is appropriate for groups that will be thinking of missionary outreach in this session. Most of our inner-city groups will not be ready to tell others much about the good news of God's love until they have had more experiences of love and have come to know

68

Jesus as the one who helped people to know God's love. An interpretation of Genesis 1:26-31 would highlight the conversation about the difference between bugs and people.

# SCHEDULE

**Cafeteria activities:** The children can begin the morning as usual with cafeteria activities. A small group may choose to illustrate the song chart, "God Is the Loving Father." The teacher who supervises this work may use the suggestions for conversation in Plan 10 of the primary textbook and choose the child who has contributed most to the conversation to bring the gist of it to the other children during the worship period at the end of the morning. After the song chart has been illustrated, it may be hung in the worship place. Activity Sheet No. 11 may be placed in the worship center too.

**Group time:** If the room and the displays are ready for the party, after the usual transition period you may want to introduce the idea of bug collecting to enliven the discussion suggested in the primary textbook and help the children to think about our belief that God gave us minds and the power to choose what we will do.

Read the suggestions in the Resource Section of this book about nature study in the inner city. It won't take long for the children to collect a few crawling things. Let them observe the bugs for a while — see how they act when a stick is placed in front of them — see what they do with a crumb.

Then help the children look from the wonder and miracle of the bug's instincts to the greater wonder and miracle of human beings as God has created them — with power to evaluate and choose what they will do, to control their instincts rather than give in to them blindly as the insects do.

Relate the observations of the children to the stories "Ramscallion" or "A Friend to the Dogs" in the story section of this book (pages 99 and 88). Talk about how hard it is to keep from grabbing food when you are hungry, and how grabbing often gets to be a habit so that you grab even when you are not hungry.

What are the perils of acting without thinking? What about walking across the street dreamily without looking for cars? Do bugs and caterpillars think before they act, or do they just go blindly ahead in any direction that is open to them? When children get a dime from their parents do they always spend it right away?

What is the difference between passing fancies and deep desires? Do children ever save their dimes even when they are hungry for ice cream because they want something else more? Isn't this hard to do? What makes them able to do it? Can a bug do something like this? An ant? A dog?

Animals can be trained sometimes to wait before they do something or take something they want, but this is because their trainer gives them a reward or punishment, not because they think and decide inside themselves what they will do. People are different. God has made us with the power to control our own actions. We can think about the value of an ice cream cone right now or a new ball in several weeks if we save our money. Then we can decide what we really want. Only people can do this.

We can think about the way our friends feel when we talk so much in a discussion that no one else has a turn. We can decide to wait sometimes to say what we feel like saying so that our friends will have a turn to talk and we can know them better.

This discussion may be continued to include the idea that God gave us the power to choose between a life of love and friendliness and one of unfriendliness and loneliness. It might take in the suggestion in the primary textbook that many people in the world do not know about God and his love and that missionaries go all over the world to spread the good news. If the children have brought offering money each day, or if an offering will be received when the parents visit, the children may want to dedicate this money for some special missionary project of the church.

**Worship:** Use the service of worship you plan to use at the open house party. Close with the friendship circle and the friendship song.

SECTION 3 | # general session plans

# PLAN 1

# come in!

**Purpose:** To welcome the children.

**Preparation:** Set up cafeteria activities in as tempting an array as possible. In the spirit of 1 John 4:19, "We love, because he first loved us," we must extend ourselves and our efforts to these inner-city children before we may expect anything of them in the way of cooperation or growth. See the Resource Section of this book for space-travel ideas, painting and clay work, sand and glue work. Have a teacher or an adult assistant at each interest center and allow the children to circulate freely.

**Group time:** Play a folk-song record or sit down with a guitar, ukelele, or Autoharp and sing to invite those who will to come hear a story. Allow others to continue with any work or play that absorbs them. "The Crocodile" song on page 115 in *Handbook for Recreation* will catch the children's interest. Tell the story "The Boy, the Man, and the Rocket Ship" from page 85 of this book, partly for amusement and entertainment and partly to help the children realize that there is such an accepting, challenging attitude in some people as the man in the rocket ship displayed. Discuss the story if they will. Measure the children off by height, four children of similar height to ride in each rocket ship while they have their juice and cookies. Snack-time rocket ships are made of large cardboard boxes or four chairs in a ring, placed either upside down or sideways.

**Worship:** Set up a worship center (on a chair if need be) with a picture of Jesus, a Bible, and perhaps a small flowering plant. As if you, the teachers, are missionaries in a foreign land, state your case briefly: " Mrs. Brant and I are friends. We have heard about this man, Jesus (show picture), who was the greatest friend that ever lived. He came to tell us about God and to help us think about other people as well as ourselves. Thinking about others is the first step to being a friend.

" Mrs. Brant and I want to be your friends and we want to tell you more about Jesus. We pray to God every day asking for his help to be friendly as Jesus was. Jesus said God will help you too, if you pray to him."

Then pray: " Oh, God, help us all to be great friends. Amen."

Play a recording of organ music by Schweitzer, who is a great friend of many people. Or the teachers may sing together " Oh, Master of the Loving Heart," No. 83 in *Hymns for Junior Worship,* or " Friends, Friends, Friends " from the primary textbook.

**Game:** " Button Snap " on page 57 in *Handbook for Recreation* is a good game to keep in mind during this session for a small group of children who may need a change of activity.

# PLAN 2

# a whole group of friends

**Purpose:** To establish a sense of fellowship.

**Preparation:** Be ready to teach during any close informal moments that may occur. Do not be discouraged if the children seem too restless to listen to stories or take part in Bible discussions. Remember your primary purpose is to help each child see the other children, you, and himself as persons with rights, persons worthy of respect, persons as much in need of interest, love, and help from other persons and from God as the fishermen and the Nazareth folk were in need of Jesus' ministrations.

In the company of Jesus people strive to understand, love, and help each other. It is in the company of Jesus that people are enabled to overcome human weaknesses and become true friends and neighbors. It is in this fellowship, too, that a right relationship with God begins to grow.

Have supplies ready to introduce one or more of the friendship projects described in the Resource Section of this book. Set up cafeteria activities — at least paint and clay. If you have primary children, try also to provide blocks and housekeeping equipment.

**Group time:** Sing " The Crocodile " or any folk song the children enjoyed yesterday. Perhaps rehearse the songs the teachers sang yesterday during worship so that all the children can join in them during worship today. Play the game "Little Tommy Tinker," page 116, *Handbook for Recreation*.

Enjoy the juice and cookie snack together, singing the up-and-down-the-scale "Grace" on page 107 of this book.

Show pictures of Jesus with his friends, the disciples, and perhaps tell their names. Then pick up the Bible and tell the story of "Jesus and the Bible" as outlined in the story section of this book (page 93). Afterwards perhaps talk about famous friends to all humanity that the children may have heard or read about: Schweitzer, Salk, Dooley, Marian Anderson, Ralph Bunche, Marie Curie. You might tell about some of the great Bible friends: David and Jonathan, Ruth and Naomi, Paul and Timothy.

**Worship:** Sing the song that was rehearsed for worship. Recall friendly acts that were done by or for members of the group during the morning. Ask the children to close their eyes and remember these or other friendly deeds they may know about. After a moment of silence conclude the meditative moment with a spoken prayer: "Thank you, God, for all our friends, for the kind and thoughtful things they do. Help us in our work and play to be kind and thoughtful and friendly too. Amen."

Introduce the friendship circle and the friendship song in the Resource Section of this book, page 107.

# the way things are and the way they might be

**Purpose:** To inspire Christian courage and trust.

**Preparation:** Invite someone to visit who has taken a close look at things as they are and worked hard to make them come nearer to what they might be. The director of a neighborhood settlement house might tell of his work and of the people who finance it. A policeman with a sense of vocation might tell his life story and why he chose law enforcement. (He must be a sincere protector of human rights, however. Inner-city children are too often aware of the fact that some policemen are in the job for what they can get out of it; not to serve their fellowmen in justice and mercy.)

Or you might plan a trip. Go to a park, to the woods or to a beach, just to give the children the joy of knowing there is another kind of place in the world — something to dream about, something to hope for, something to work toward.

If the children are to play in the woods or on a crowded beach with other people, it may be well to provide your group with strips of bright-colored cambric to wear over the shoulder and attached to the belt or as an arm band. Such bright strips make the children easy to identify in crowds and easy to see at a distance.

**Group time:** Sing choruses of " The Poor Old World " and " It Could Be a Wonderful World " from *Little Songs on Big Subjects* (see bibliography, page 118).

The picture-storybook *The Skyscraper* by Yen Liang (described in the Resource Section of this book) may lead to a discussion of the way things are and the way they might be and what we can do to change things. Courage and hope may come to inner-city children if they know that some people are planning and working sacrificially for city improvements.

In the area of relationships we must deal with the hopelessness some inner-city people feel because of rejection. We must somehow convince the children that at least in the church, at least by you the teacher, they are fully accepted. This is a needed step toward the understanding and acceptance of the love of God. Perhaps within the group the children themselves have begun to feel accepted by each other. Perhaps at discussion time tales of welcoming experiences have been recounted. Perhaps a child has told how he felt in making someone else feel welcome or included. At such times we may help the children see how things could be between people and enlist their enthusiasm in the interest of friendliness.

In some city neighborhoods we must not go too far in this direction, however. It is not safe in some places to encourage attitudes of unlimited trust in children by assuring them that " a friend is inside each person they meet, everywhere on every street." We must be realistic and help them distinguish their friends from narcotics peddlers, sex deviants, and a great variety of other exploiters of children. (Still it is the Christian hope and faith that even in these unfortunate creatures there is the capacity to respond to the love of God from whom they have been estranged.)

Read the two story incidents " Manolo, a Friend? " (page 98) and " Pete, the Paper Boy " (page 99). Then ask the children to make up a story called " Manolo, a Friend "–without the question mark.

**Worship:** Tell " The Story of Jesus' Ministry " (page 94), sing " It Could Be a Wonderful World," and pray: " O most loving God, we are glad to know about Jesus and how he loved and helped people. We remember how he told everyone to pray for help. We ask you now to make us see what we can do to change what needs to be changed in our lives so that your love can come to us and make us strong and loving too. Amen."

# PLAN 4

# the best things in life are free

**Purpose:** To stimulate evaluation of the good things in our world.

**Preparation:** Buy or make a good supply of price tags large enough so that a ten-word phrase can be written on them. Arrange with another group in the vacation church school for the children to come and " buy " what your group is " selling," Decide upon a place where the " store " can be set up.

**Group time:** Begin the day with the story " A Shopping Spree " (page 101). This story should start the children thinking about things that make their lives rich and full, yet are available without money. Everything has a price, however, even if it is only awareness. The discussion after the story should include moments of meditation about the price of a friend, the cost of being part of a group or a family. Older children may carry the discussion on to the point where privileges and responsibilities are considered as two sides of the same coin.

When a number of " free " things have been listed with their " prices," the children can begin to symbolize them with paint or clay in any way they choose. They may paint or model such things as:

79

| ITEM | PRICE |
|------|-------|
| A SMILE | a smile |
| A LAUGH | a joke well told |
| A FRIEND | kindness and understanding |
| A PAL | willingness to do the things *he* wants to do sometimes |
| CLEAN HANDS | a few minutes' washing |
| A HAPPY MOTHER | errands done willingly |
| BOOKS TO READ | a six-block walk to library |

Prices should be written on the tags which are then attached to the pictures or the modeling. When the articles are placed in the store the tags are turned face down so that the buyers will be surprised.

After the children in the group have set up the store and gone shopping for each other's merchandise they may send a representative to invite another group in the vacation church school to come and buy. These children may be invited to worship with your group too.

**Worship:** Begin with the song " All Things to Enjoy " Viola W. Franklin's musical setting for 1 Timothy 6:17 (from *Sing, Children, Sing*). Then make up a litany of the things the children have put in the store.

The child who has made a rainbow, for instance, may hold it up and say, " For rainbows we may see for a look out the window."

Then the children together will say, " We thank you, God."

Another child may hold up a picture of a boy showing the muscles in his arm and say, " For new strength after a good night's sleep."

Then the children together will say, " We thank you, God."

**Games:** Games for the day should be those which help to sharpen the senses, such as the touching game. A bag is filled with various things — a wad of cotton, a sponge, a clothespin, a stick of gum, a key, a safety pin, and the like. Each child is given a minute to feel the things inside the bag. Then he is told to list them.

A variation of this is the smelling game. Under the nose of a child who is blindfolded another child holds a fresh flower, a cup of vinegar, a cut-open apple, a piece of cheese, perfume, library paste, or other items with distinctive odors. The blindfolded child guesses what it is that he is smelling.

# PLAN 5

# doing what
# we thought
# we couldn't do

**Purpose:** To discover new depths in ourselves.

**Preparation:** If your children are too young to write readily, bring a
pile of old magazines so that they may find pictures in them which
will illustrate the things they want to learn to do, to be, to work for.
Sheets of brown paper should be cut, folded, and stapled together
to make booklets, one for each child to decorate and fill in as he likes.

Since this is to be a personal evaluation, the children may want
to keep the books secret. If so, spread the group out for the work.
Give each child his own "island" to work in, even if it is only a
chalked circle on the floor.

Pages or sections of the books should be marked in the following
categories:

Things I know I can do well
Things I'd like to learn to do well
Things I have to do but don't like very much
People who do things the way I'd like to do them

81

**Group time:** Tell the story "Limp the Chimp" (page 95). After the story ask the children to make an evaluation booklet together, such as Limp might have made for himself at the beginning of the story. Then discuss questions such as these: What made Limp able to do things he thought he couldn't do? Have you ever done something you thought you couldn't do? What made you able to do it? How does it feel when you finally learn to judge distance and to keep your balance so that you can jump through a whole hop-scotch game without landing on a single line? How does it feel to catch a fly ball? Or hit a home run? Doesn't the whole world look different when you've learned to play ball well enough so that the gang wants you to play with them? Doesn't the whole world seem a better place to be in when you have learned to do something new? Do people like *you* more when you have learned to do something? Do you like *them* more?

Perhaps in the discussion one child will reveal a previously concealed desire to learn a skill. Perhaps the group can give him courage by telling about how they learned it or the troubles they had and how they overcame them. Perhaps the children can go off in teams to help each other learn things such as stilt walking, catching or batting balls, handspring turning, whistling, painting, clay modeling, or reading.

**Worship:** Tell about the difficult things Jesus had to do and how often he reminded people that with God's help many hard things can be accomplished. Recall things done by famous people in spite of handicaps. (Glen Cunningham, the track star, suffered serious burns as a child and the doctors said he might never walk again; George Washington Carver, the distinguished scientist, never knew his real name but had to make up one; Louis Pasteur, another famous scientist, was a cripple.) Read Matthew 19:26 together. Sing "I'm Proud to Be Me" (page 44 in the junior pupil's book). Express thanks to God, the great creator and provider.

**Game:** Arrange an obstacle course with chairs and tables to climb over. Divide the group into teams of two. Blindfold each member in turn and let the other member of his team be his eyes to guide him over the course. Afterwards talk about our many skills and powers that we take for granted when we should be holding them in high esteem and gratefulness to God, our creator.

# SECTION 4 | resources

# The Boy, the Man, and
# the Rocket Ship

*(This story may speak hopefully to the feelings of inade-
quacy and rejection so prevalent in the inner city.)*

Once upon a time a Man made a Rocket Ship. He said, " I am going
to visit the planets. Who will go with me? "

" I will go with you," said the Boy.

" Oh, you are too small! " said the People.

But the Man looked at the Boy. He said, " You are growing bigger
all the time and we'll be gone for many years. You are big enough
to go."

Then the People said, " He doesn't know enough."

The Man looked at the Boy again. " Can you listen when somebody
tells you something? " he asked. " Can you keep your eyes wide open
to see what there is to see? Can you think? "

" Yes! " said the Boy.

" Then even if you don't know enough now, you can learn," said
the Man. " Come along! "

*Bang! Swoosh!* And away they went.

It was a long, hard trip. The Man had to study his charts, take instrument readings, consult the check list, and do a million other things
almost all the time. But while he worked he talked out loud. The
Boy kept his ears and his eyes open. He learned many things about
rocket ships. The Man taught him to play checkers too, in their spare
time whenever the rocket ship was sailing smoothly instead of bump-
ing around the way it did sometimes.

Finally they could see a planet just ahead. But when they were
close enough they could see that the people didn't want them. Bright
lights were turned on the rocket ship; the glare was so bad they
couldn't see where to land. There were buzzing noises and explosions.
They had to turn away.

The Boy started to cry. The Man wasn't very happy either. But he said, "Who cares? There are plenty of other places to go." And he began to study the charts again.

The Boy looked over his shoulder. He saw a mark that showed where they could find another planet.

"Could we go to that planet?" he asked.

"Good idea!" said the Man. And they headed that way.

This time the Boy helped the Man read the charts, take instrument readings, consult the check list, and do the million other things that had to be done. He was learning all the time. And sometimes when the ship was sailing smoothly, he beat the Man at checkers.

The people on the second planet didn't want them either, but by this time the Boy knew how to study charts almost as well as the Man. He knew how many places there were to go in the universe. This time he didn't cry.

The Man and the Boy landed safely on the next planet. When they stepped out of the rocket ship to look around, they saw people running toward them. The Boy moved closer to the Man. Some of the people carried weapons and scowled fiercely. Others looked them over with great curiosity. A few even smiled in a friendly way. The Man and the Boy smiled at everybody and explained that they were friends from the Earth.

They made quite a long visit on that planet. Then the Man said to the Boy, "Shall we go?"

The Boy nodded, "Yes!" And away they went to another planet.

They took turns choosing where they would head for. First the Boy picked a planet and then the Man picked one. Sometimes the people wanted them to land and sometimes they didn't. Wherever they landed, somebody wanted a ride.

The Boy would ask, "Can you listen when somebody tells you something? Can you keep your eyes wide open to see what there is to see? Can you think?" And if the answer was, "Yes," he would say, "Come along!"

On the long, hard trips from planet to planet he showed them how to study the charts and take instrument readings and navigate by the stars. And in their spare time, when the rocket ship was sailing smoothly, they would play checkers.

One time they headed the rocket back to the Earth for a while. When they landed, the People waved flags and whistled whistles and paraded in parades. They didn't even remember they had said the Boy was too small and didn't know enough to go.

# The Biggest and Best

*(There is deprivation in the inner city that must be endured, but children often feel needlessly deprived because of the excessive boastfulness of some of their companions. It is good for children to look into their lives for heretofore taken-for-granted values.)*

For a long time Millie had not had anyone her own age to play with. Only boys and very small children lived on her street. Finally a girl moved in. She was just Millie's age.

A few days later Millie was watching her mother iron her father's shirts. "Why don't you go outside and play with your new friend? " her mother asked.

"I don't think I want to be her friend," said Millie.

"Why not? " said Mother.

Millie didn't know exactly. She went outside to see how Rose would act today.

"Hello, Millie," said Rose. "See my new bike? Don't you wish you had one? " And she went riding down the street on it.

The day before Rose had said, " Hello, Millie. See my new sweater? It has my initials on it." Millie's sweater didn't have even buttons on it.

The day before that it had been, " Hello, Millie. See my new ring? It's my own." And Rose had put her hand in her pocket so that Millie couldn't even touch the ring.

Today Millie went back into the house and sat on the kitchen stool again. Her mother was ironing dresses now.

"Rose has everything, and I don't have anything big or good or different," Millie complained.

"Well, you know," said her mother, " Mr. Jones said you could have that kitten when he grew big enough to leave his mother."

"But I don't have it now," said Millie.

Her mother made the iron go back and forth, back and forth, over Millie's pink Sunday dress.

"I know something you have that's so big you could give some to Rose and still have plenty for yourself," said her mother.

Millie almost fell off the stool, she was so excited. "What is it? What is it? " she asked.

Her mother whispered something in her ear. Millie jumped down and ran outside to find Rose.

"Hello, Rose," said Millie. "I've got something so big I can give some to you and still have plenty for myself."

Rose guessed and guessed. She couldn't think what it was that Millie had.

"Come along. I'll show you," Millie said.

They walked down the street and turned the corner. Then they walked down another street. A great big church stood there, the one Millie went to every Sunday with her mother and father.

They walked right up to the church and Millie took Rose inside. It was cool and quiet and beautiful. Millie showed Rose the flowers there. She took her upstairs where the children's rooms were.

"See how big my church is? " Millie said to Rose. "It can be your church too, if you want to belong. But it will still be mine! "

# A Friend to the Dogs

*(This story can be used to help children think about instincts and free choice and the joy and privilege of being able to decide what they will do and what they will not do.)*

Nobody could make Juan do anything he didn't want to do. He ran past the fruit and vegetable store and knocked a basket of potatoes off the corner of the shelf that Mr. Josetti had built. Mr. Josetti yelled, "You come back here, you, and pick up my potatoes! " But Juan kept on running.

"Go home, Juan! Your mother wants you," called Mary. The girls who were walking down the street with her giggled. They all called after him. "Go home, Juan! Your mother wants you." But Juan kept on running. Nobody could make him do anything he didn't want to do.

He ran and ran until he was out of breath. He sat down on the curbstone near the place where men were putting up the big tent for the circus. There were trailers parked all around. The circus people lived in the trailers. Some great big ones, like moving vans, had animals in them. A smaller one was full of little cages with a little white dog in each cage. That was the trailer Juan liked best.

" Yip, yip, yip! Yipe, yipe, yipe! " barked the little dogs.

" Shut up! " said Juan, but they didn't. They put their little wet noses through the slats in the cages and sniffed at his hand and then they yip, yip, yipped and yipe, yipe, yiped some more.

" Hey, get away from there! " yelled a man. Juan didn't move. Nobody could make him do anything he didn't want to do. He stood perfectly still.

" Can't you hear me? " said the man coming toward Juan. " I said get away from my dogs."

Juan stood perfectly still, looking at the dogs.

" All right then," said the man. " Maybe you don't understand English. I'll get the dogs away from *you*." He opened every little box-cage and let out all the dogs. They jumped around him and wagged their tails and yiped until it sounded as if there were a million dogs instead of only ten.

The man whistled and they stopped barking. He looked at Juan again. " Maybe you don't understand English, and maybe you do. I'll give you a quarter when I come back if all those cages have been brushed out with the brush hanging here, and if all the water dishes inside are filled with fresh water from the tank over there."

Then he turned and walked away. The dogs ran after him, yiping and yipping and fluttering around the man's legs like pieces of white paper swirling around in the wind.

Nobody could make Juan do anything he didn't want to do, but he wanted to do this. He went to work right away and brushed out the cages. He rinsed out the water dishes and filled them with fresh water. Then he ran along the path where the man and the dogs had gone.

They were out of sight, but he thought he could hear the dogs yipping. He followed the sound between trailers and cars and trucks to the very edge of the big circus tent. A flap was open. In he went and found the man and his dogs practising their circus act.

First the dogs scrambled and yiped around the man's legs. Then he whistled. In a minute they were all sitting up on little red barrels around the edge of the ring. The man whistled again in a different way and stood near one dog with a hoop in his hand. The dog jumped through the hoop and then trotted back to his barrel. After every dog had done this trick, the man went around the ring feeding each one a treat.

One dog didn't wait, but jumped off his barrel before the man came to him. The man flicked a little whip at this dog. The dog said, " *Yiiiiiiiiipe!* " and went back to his place. He stayed there then, even if he didn't get anything to eat.

" He couldn't make me do that," said Juan to himself. " He couldn't make me do anything I didn't want to do." But was he sure the little dog didn't want to do what the man wanted him to do?

When the man whistled again, all the dogs jumped down. He sat on a barrel in the middle of the ring and let them scramble around him. He rubbed their ears and patted them and let them jump up on his lap and off again. All the time they yipped and yiped as if they were laughing. Juan thought it must feel good to have somebody rub your ears and pat you like that.

Then the man whistled again. The dogs stopped yipping and jumped back on their barrels. He began to teach them a new trick. He started them all running in a big circle. The second dog was supposed to jump over the first, and the third dog over the first and second, and the fourth dog over the first and the second and the third.

This trick was hard to learn. The little whip flicked again and again. Only one dog got something to eat. They were all panting and their tongues were hanging out. " He couldn't make me do that," said Juan to himself. But the little dogs kept trying.

At last the man whistled again and started to walk out of the tent toward the cages. He didn't pay any attention to the dogs. They could have run away if they had wanted to. But they didn't. They went after him, yiping and yipping.

Juan followed them. He saw each dog jump into one of the cages he had cleaned. He saw them lap up the cool water he had put there for them.

The man came to Juan, smiling. " Here's your pay," he said. " I see you do understand English after all."

Juan wanted the dogs to stop yiping so he could hear what the man was saying. " Shut up! " he yelled, but they didn't. The man whistled and they were quiet.

" Why do they do things for you even when they don't want to? " asked Juan.

" Oh, they do want to," said the man. " I'm their friend, you see! "

All the way home with the quarter in his pocket Juan was wondering what it means to be a friend. Does it mean to whip people and give them things to eat that they like? Or is being a friend to a dog different from being a friend to a person? How do you get *people* to do things for you that they don't want to do?

# The Girl

*(This story might be used to interest the children in mosaic work of some kind. It might help the children get a hint of the warm pleasure that comes with human companionship.)*

Juan found the girl one day when he was running away from Manolo. He was going to go back and run after Manolo again in a little while, but now he needed a rest. He turned down an alley and discovered a door in a fence. It opened on a sandy lot.

A girl was there, sitting on the ground. She jumped up and started to run away when Juan came through the door.

"I won't hurt you," said Juan quickly. He flopped on the ground, flat on his stomach, too tired and out of breath to move. The girl sat down again and began putting things in a little hole she had dug.

"What are you doing?" asked Juan, lifting his head to see. He dragged himself closer by digging his elbows into the ground and inching forward on them.

The girl didn't say a word. She had a little box with colored things in it – little pieces of glass, different-colored strings, broken bits of plastic, rusty nails and screws and bolts, and shiny bottle caps. She was putting them into the bottom of a square hole she had dug. The ground there was sticky like clay and the things stayed where she wanted them. She was making a design, something that looked like lightning, with pieces of red and green glass put into a zigzag pattern. When the sun came out from behind a cloud her design glittered.

Juan rested and watched for a long time. Then the sun went behind a cloud and stayed there. The girl put a cover on her box and carefully sprinkled over her design some of the sandy dirt that was on top of the ground. Soon the ground was all level so no one could see there had been a hole. She stood up and looked at Juan for a minute, then ran away.

Juan thought she was crazy. " What's she doing that for? " he wondered. But for days after that, whenever he saw a piece of colored glass or something shiny, he picked it up and put it into his pocket. One day he found a long cardboard tube with a cover. After that he kept the little bits of colored things in there.

When the tube was nearly full, Juan tried to find the alley with the door in the fence that opened on the lot. He found the place, but the girl was not there. He flopped down on his stomach and tried to remember exactly where the hole was that she had covered. But he couldn't remember.

He didn't hear a sound, but all of a sudden there she was digging near the fence. She dug up a little brush buried in the ground. Then she began to brush away the sand in one spot until the hole he had seen her working in was all uncovered. The lightning design was red and green and yellow now, and all around it were bits of clear glass. It was like a picture in the ground. The girl began to work on it again, putting back pieces that she had brushed away with the sand and adding new pieces to the design. She didn't look at Juan.

He took out the cardboard tube and pushed it toward her. " Here," he said, " you can have it." When she didn't touch it, he took the cover off and spilled out some of the colored things.

The girl looked at him then, but still she didn't say anything. She took the brush and went to a different part of the lot. She uncovered another hole, and when Juan went to see, there was another picture. This one had a little round mirror in the center. Around it were rings and rings of colored things. Around these were points. After Juan had seen it, she covered it up and showed him another picture. The whole place was full of surprises.

Then the girl went back to work on the lightning picture, never saying a word. The first time she took some pieces out of the treasures Juan had brought, she looked at his face as if to be sure he meant for her to have them. He nodded, and after that she just kept working, not looking up at all, until she had finished the picture and covered it. Before she ran away, she looked at Juan's face again.

Juan never found out where the girl lived. He never knew her name or talked with her. But after that, no matter how fast he was running or where he was going, he always stopped to pick up a bit of something that was shiny or bright-colored. And he spent many happy hours in that sandy lot watching the girl work.

He wondered if they were friends.

# Jesus and the Bible

*(Introductory remarks to children who may have had little or no Bible background.)*

Jesus came to tell us that God loves everybody, even the ones some people say are "no good." All people do wrong things sometimes, and some people think God stops loving them because of this. Jesus said, "No, God never stops loving. He is always ready to help anyone who tries to follow his way of living and loving."

This part of the Bible (hold up a Bible open at the Gospels) tells how Jesus came to show us God's way of living and loving. There are many wonderful stories telling how God's strength and love came to people through Jesus. There was a man who had been sick for a long time. After he had talked about God with Jesus, he felt strong enough to get up off his mat, lift it to his shoulders, and walk away. There was another man who had been a cheat and was very lonely because he thought no one wanted to be his friend. He hid in a tree when Jesus came to his town. Jesus called him down from the tree and told him they would have lunch together. When this man saw that Jesus wanted to be his friend and found out that God still loved him, he stopped cheating and became honest. God's strength began to work in him, helping him do things he thought he never could do.

Jesus made friends of some men who thought all they could do was fish. As they listened to Jesus and thought about God and prayed for strength, they began to be able to do other things. They traveled all over the country and talked about God before big crowds of people.

It seems that people are only half alive until they know God loves them and they begin to love him and other people. Jesus said, "Do this, and you will live."

There is no end to what God's love and strength can help you do. Sometimes, with his help, you can even be a friend to somebody nobody else likes. You can teach him what it is to be loved himself and what it is to love God and other people.

# The Story of Jesus' Ministry

*(This is not really a story. It is the way one teacher told about Jesus in her own words, from the parts of the Bible that had most meaning for her. Your story may vary as you tell it to your pupils.)*

Today it happens to be hot and sunny here in the city. In the country of Palestine it is almost always hot and sunny. That is where Jesus lived when he came to tell people the good news of God's love.

There were rich people and poor people then too. There were people who found it hard to do the right thing. There were people who had never even thought about what was right and what was wrong. There were people who knew what was right and what was wrong and did wrong anyway because they didn't think it made any difference. (Pause if you see a child who might tell of someone he knows who is like this. If you look into the faces of the children as you tell a story, you can see immediately when what you say strikes a response.)

Jesus himself did not have a big, rich house, expensive clothes, or anything like that. What he had was much more valuable than those things. He knew God. He knew people weren't really as bad as they looked or as they thought they were. He knew most of them didn't really want to be the way they were. He told them how God could help them change themselves from bad, sad, sick, unfriendly people into friendly, loving, helpful people. Then, he said, they would begin to make things the way they *could* be.

It was as if he had taken a big, strong searchlight and turned it in a new direction to show a street that hadn't been seen before. Some people went down that street. Some people decided not to, and they continued to be sad or sick or sorry for themselves.

Jesus knew he wouldn't be able to talk to all the people in the world, face to face, through all the years. But he told people that when he was gone, God would keep on sending comfort and wisdom and strength and love. He said that whenever two or three of them were together praying and thinking about his way for them, then God would help by making them see the right thing to do and the right way to go.

# Limp the Chimp

*(Some inner-city children are lax, hopeless, and unwilling
to make an effort to further their own welfare or happiness.)*

In the jungle there was a deep, dark cave where the King of the Beasts lived. He was so old he never went out any more, and he had been in there so long that nobody could remember how he looked. But everyone remembered how wise he was. When any animal was in trouble, he was advised to go to the King of the Beasts.

Now there was a young chimpanzee who was never merry and gay. All he did was wander around. He never felt peppy enough even to get fresh food to eat.

"That's such hard work," he said. "So much climbing way up in the tall trees! So much throwing to break the coconut shells open!"

Limp the Chimp they called him.

All he did was wander around, picking up leftover pieces of bananas and coconuts.

Everyone else would get so tired of climbing and throwing that when afternoon came they would stretch out in the sunshine and take a good long nap. After that they would play together, merry and gay.

But not Limp the Chimp. He was very sad.

"You are in trouble," they told him. "Go to the King of the Beasts." And he did.

"What's your trouble?" asked the King. His voice came out of the cave with a roar and a rumble that made the leaves tremble.

"I don't know," said Limp the Chimp.

"Well," said the King, and his voice came out of the cave like an explosion. "I can't help you with your trouble unless you know what your your trouble is. Go ask your friends."

"I have no friends," said Limp the Chimp.

"What? No friends?" asked the King. "Who sent you here?"

"Oh, those were just chimpanzees," said Limp. "Just the ones I see every day."

"Do you know what a friend is?" asked the King.

"Oh, yes," answered Limp the Chimp.

"What is a friend? Tell me what you think a friend is," said the King.

The chimp couldn't say a word. He had thought he knew, but when it came right down to telling about it, he didn't.

" Go back! " ordered the King. " Get busy. Don't come to me again until you can tell me what a friend is. Shoo! Whoo! " His voice came out of the cave with a thunder and a wind that sent the chimp on his way faster than he had ever traveled. It was as if someone had given him a big shove from behind.

"Whew! " he thought to himself as he swung along on a branch and then ran for a few steps until he could catch on to another branch and swing again. " Whew! But I kind of like traveling at this speed! "

He didn't slow down until he came to the river. There he took a long cold drink. It tasted so good that he looked hard at the river, wondering if some berry juice or something had got into the water. No, it was the same old river. " Guess I was just more thirsty than I usually am," he thought.

Then he began to look around for something to eat. " Can't do what the King wants me to do on an empty stomach," he said.

He looked everywhere for some leftovers. Not a single broken coconut shell could he find that had even a scrap left in it to eat. Not a tiny piece of banana. Not even any banana peelings.

" Oh, dear," he said. " I can't wait for someone to eat his meal and throw the leftovers around. The King said I must get busy right away. There's nothing to do but climb a tree."

Up he went, this time without a shove from behind, lickety split to the top of the tallest coconut tree. He picked the biggest coconut he could find and, *wham*, he threw it down on the ground to crack it, using muscles he didn't know he had.

Then he scrambled down to drink the coconut milk before it leaked out of the shell. It was very good. He didn't have the milk often. No one gets coconut milk in leftovers – only little bits of coconut meat that happen to be left in the shell after somebody has had a good meal out of it.

He drank all the milk and ate all the coconut. When he had finished, there wasn't a speck left over. He took a deep breath and looked up. Why, a little white monkey was watching him!

" Oh," said the monkey. " I hoped you'd leave me just a few crumbs. I've twisted my arm and bruised my leg and I can't climb at all today."

" Just a minute," said Limp. " I'll go up and get another coconut." Lickety split, up he went. *Wham! Bam!* Down came a coconut. The little white monkey had to scramble to get out of the way. Then down came Limp the Chimp.

" Help yourself," he said to the monkey. " I've had mine."

" This is very good of you," said the monkey, " to go up there just for me."

" Oh, well," said Limp, " I have some muscles I didn't know I had. I think I'd better exercise them. Do you want another coconut?"

" No, thank you. This one was delicious and I feel much better. I'll have to be getting along now. Good-by, Friend." And he went on his way.

" Wait! Wait! " shouted Limp. " What was that you called me? "

The little monkey stopped and turned around. " Why, I called you Friend," he answered. " I said, ' Good-by, Friend.' "

" What is a friend? " asked Limp. " Tell me, what is a friend? "

" Well, you are one," said the little monkey. " A friend is someone who helps you when you need help and you certainly helped me. So I'll say it again, ' Good-by, Friend,' and thank you." Then away he scrambled into the bushes because he couldn't run and swing in the trees because of his bruises.

Limp the Chimp went along swinging and running. Suddenly he felt very merry and gay!

" Who's that swinging and running along, looking so merry and gay? " asked Nimp. She was throwing little nuts at Skimp, and he was chasing her up and down the trees.

" I don't know," said Skimp. " I never saw him before . . . why, it's Limp! Look at him go! "

" Hey, Limp! " he called, and he threw a nut at him. Then he pulled Nimp behind a tree trunk where they couldn't be seen. When Limp came near, looking around, they both jumped out to surprise him. All three rolled over and over down the hill until they were out of breath.

" What's happened to you? " they asked Limp. " We didn't even recognize you! "

Limp told them about the King of the Beasts and the little monkey and how he had discovered the muscles he didn't know he had, when he had climbed the tree for a coconut.

" You have some other friends, too, that you didn't know you had," Nimp told him, winking at Skimp.

" You mean — you? " asked Limp.

" Why, sure," they said. And they chased him up a tree.

# Manolo — a Friend?

*(Some people seem friendly. But are they real friends?)*

Nobody could make Juan do anything he didn't want to do — nobody but a friend. "Shut up, you kids," yelled old Jake. Juan and the other boys just went on whooping it up.

But "C'mon along, Juan," said his new friend Manolo, and right off Juan left the fun and they walked down the street together. Manolo always had plans for things to do. He always had surprises in his pockets.

"What's in your pocket today?" asked Juan. "Chocolate bars? A new glider? Where do you get all the stuff? Does your mother own a store or something?"

Manolo just smiled and pulled his pocket inside out to show he had nothing. "If I had something, I'd give it to you," he said, "but I know where we can get something."

"Where, where?" asked Juan. "Let's go. I'm hungry."

That's when the trouble started. Manolo took Juan up this street and down that to another neighborhod where nobody knew them. All the time he was telling his plan to Juan, but quietly, so that no one would hear them.

Juan didn't like the plan. "My mother says we have to pay for everything we take," he said. "It costs the store people something too."

"Who's your friend?" asked Manolo. "Is your mother?"

Well, that made Juan feel all mixed up. His mother was his mother. Could she be a friend too?

He walked along and tried to think about it so that he wouldn't feel all mixed up. But he was still mixed up when he saw they were in front of the candy bars in the ten-cent store.

"Take one," whispered Manolo. "There's nobody here." He shoved Juan's elbow and candy bars fell all over the floor. People stood still and looked at them.

"Beat it!" said Manolo. They both started to run. They ran and ran until Juan was panting like the circus dogs.

Then Manolo gave him a good punch. "You're not my friend any more," he said. "Beat it!"

Juan began to run again, even if he was panting. As he ran he wondered if Manolo knew what it means to be a friend.

# Pete, the Paper Boy

When Juan thought of his friends, he always thought of Pete, the paper boy. Pete wasn't really a boy. He was a little man with a hook for one hand and a stick of wood for one leg.

One day Pete saw Manolo punch Juan. He left his paper stand and chased after the boy. Pete was smaller than Manolo, but when he waved the hook and stumped after him, Manolo ran away fast. Then Pete came back to his papers.

"I guess he's afraid of your hook," said Juan, spitting out blood. The punch had made his lip bleed. Pete gave him a piece of clean paper to hold against his mouth.

"And what are *you* afraid of, hey?" Pete asked him.

Juan guessed he was afraid of Manolo when Manolo was mad at him.

"You, with two good arms?" exclaimed Pete. "And two strong kicking legs!"

Juan looked at his arms and his legs. They were strong. "But I'm not as big as Manolo," he said. "Pete, you know how big he is. He's bigger than I am."

"Maybe so," said Pete. "Maybe so. But he's bigger than I am too. And didn't he run when I chased him? Manolo shouldn't have punched you. No matter how big they are, if they hurt somebody, I chase them. And they always run!"

Juan wondered and wondered why this was so.

# Ramscallion

"My, how big you're getting to be!"

That's what Mamscallion, the mother lion, said one day. "My, how big you're getting to be, Ramscallion! You're certainly growing every day. Are you learning something every day too?"

"Watch me pounce!" said Ramscallion. He crouched down low on his legs. His tail went swish-swish, this way and that, this way and that. Then up he jumped, up in the air, and landed *pow!* Whatever it was he landed on was squashed flatter than a pancake, and so he ate it like a pancake. He went back to his mother, licking his chops.

" My, how you can pounce! " said his mother, " But what was that you ate? "

"I don't know," said Ramscallion. "I saw something moving. I pounced, and it was squashed flatter than a pancake. So I ate it."

" Were you hungry? " asked his mother.

" No, not exactly," said Ramscallion.

"Well," said his mother, " you certainly are growing, you certainly can pounce, and you certainly have a great deal to learn! "

Ramscallion wondered and wondered about that.

" My, how big you're getting to be! "

That is what Mamscallion, the mother lion, said on another day. " My, how big you're getting to be, Ramscallion! You're certainly growing every day. Are you learning something every day too? "

" Watch me pounce! " said Ramscallion. He crouched down low on his legs. His tail went swish-swish, this way and that, this way and that. Then up he jumped, up in the air, and landed *pow!* Whatever it was he landed on was squashed flatter than a pancake, but Ramscallion didn't eat it. Not this time! He wasn't hungry.

" My, how you can pounce! " said his mother. " But what was that you pounced on? "

" I don't know," said Ramscallion. " I didn't really look. I saw something moving, I pounced, and it was squashed flatter than a pancake. But I wasn't hungry, so I didn't eat it."

" Well," said his mother, " you certainly can pounce, you certainly are learning a little, but there is still a great deal more to learn."

Ramscallion wondered and wondered about that.

" When I see something moving, *pow!* I pounce," Ramscallion said to himself. " Then I can't tell the difference between it, whatever it was, and a pancake. I'll have to stop and look before I pounce. That's what I'll have to do."

So he did. Every time he saw something moving, he stopped to think if he was hungry or not. If he was hungry, *pow!* he pounced and *yum!* he ate. If he wasn't hungry, he just crouched down low on his legs and his tail went swish-swish, this way and that, this way and that, but he didn't jump up in the air to pounce. Not this time! He just looked and looked.

One day he saw a red fox with a tail that was even swishier than his own. Another day he saw a black and white striped zebra. And

once a giraffe with a long thin neck. Another time two deer, one with antlers and one without antlers.

Then one day he saw something that made him want to get closer. He straightened up his legs and made his tail stop swishing. He crept closer and closer on his soft paws. He didn't make a sound. When he was very, very close — closer than he had ever been to something that was not squashed flat — he saw that it was another lion! Another lion almost exactly his size!

" Why, hello! " said Ramscallion, and they began to play together.

Mamscallion came along and saw them playing together.

"Hello, Mother," said Ramscallion. " This is my friend, Jamscallion."

"Hello, Jamscallion! " said Ramscallion's mother. She looked at the two friends now standing side by side, " My, Ramscallion," she said, "how big you're getting to be! You have certainly grown and you have certainly learned a lot."

# A Shopping Spree

" I need a nickel. I need a dime," Marianna would say every day to her father. Sometimes she would say, " I need a quarter," or " I need fifty cents."

She bought comic books and candy, crayons and little dolls, balls and rubber bands, and jacks and things. But she always needed more. The crayons would get broken and lost, the arms of the dolls would come off, and the comic books would tear. There wouldn't be a *thing* to *do*. Marianna would have to go to her father again and say, " I need a nickel. I need a dime."

One day her father went away and didn't come home. When Marianna would ask her mother for money, her mother would say, " What do you think? I am not made of money." So Marianna had to hunt for the broken crayons and fix the dolls and piece together the comic books.

At last there was nothing left. Absolutely nothing. And there was nothing to do. Absolutely nothing. Marianna just sat at the window and moped until she fell asleep.

She dreamed that the white cloud she had been watching from the window came down and wrapped itself around her like soft cotton. Then it went floating up, up, up into the blue again and took her for a ride high into the sky.

She got off in front of a big store in the sky. The windows were full of the strangest things! Not a single crayon or doll or ball or comic book! Marianna still didn't have a bit of money, but she thought she'd just go in and look around.

Inside there was nothing to see on the counters or shelves, but store people were standing all around waiting for customers.

"May I show you something?" asked a little round man with twinkly eyes like Christmas-tree lights.

"Oh, I'm just looking. I haven't any money," said Marianna.

"*You* can pay for *our* things." said the little man. "Come with me." He whisked Marianna through a little door. *Ziiiinnnnggg!* There was a ringing in her ears and they were back in her own house. She was looking through the window again, only this time it was in the middle of the night.

"Here, wouldn't you like to buy these to look at?" asked the little man. He showed her some stars in a piece of the black night-time sky — a big shining star and several little, twinkly ones.

"How much do they cost?" asked Marianna.

"Three blinks of an eye," he said, and Marianna paid for them right away.

*Ziiinnnngggg!* There was a ringing in her ears again, and she was whisked through the little door back into the big store in the sky.

This time a young lady came up to her and said in a voice that sounded like a faraway whispering, "May I show you something?" Marianna told her she didn't have any money, but again she was whisked through the little door and heard a ringing in her ears. In a minute they were on her own sidewalk on her own street. A gentle breeze was blowing. It felt cool and fresh on Marianna's cheeks. It blew her hair off her forehead and lifted it on the sides of her head. It tickled her ears just a bit.

"Would you care to buy this lovely breeze?" asked the young lady.

"What is the price?" asked Marianna.

"A deep breath and a sigh," said the lady, and Marianna paid for it right away.

*Ziiiinnnngggg!* She was back in the store in the sky.

A tall thin man with a jack-o-lantern smile came up to her. "May I show you something?" he asked. The same thing happened all over again, through the door and down, but this time they landed right in the middle of Marianna's kitchen.

A beam of bright sunlight came in through a hole in the window-shade. All up and down it little tiny things were sparkling and gleaming, whirling and twirling round and round like dancers.

"Wouldn't you like to buy this delightful sunbeam?" asked the tall, thin man, grinning his jack-o-lantern grin.

"How much does it cost?" asked Marianna.

"One long-drawn-out *ooooohhhhhh*," he said, and Marianna paid for it right away. "*Oooooohhhhhh*."

Up in the store again a bright young man with a shining face came toward her. This time Marianna didn't bother to say she had no money. Soon they were back in her own room, looking out the window again. "Wouldn't you like to buy this moon?" he asked. "It comes in many different shapes and sizes." As he snapped his fingers, the moon changed from a big round, silvery, shining thing to the shape of a thin curved sliver, then to something that looked like a cookie with one bite taken out of it, then to a big round orange balloon, then to a pale shadowy circle. Marianna bought all these for just two words, "Oh, look!"

A pretty lady sold Marianna sunlight on her bare legs on the first warm day of spring. The price for that was one word, "*Ahhhhhh*." Then a young man raced her around the block until she was hot and tired and thirsty. He sold her a drink of cool water for a smacking of the lips.

Marianna bought a marvelously long icicle, too, and thousands and thousands of snowflakes. She bought rainbows, silvery raindrops, cottony white clouds like the one that had floated her to the store, skies that came in as many colors as the moon came in sizes and shapes.

But she didn't spend a penny.

# When the Other Side Came Over

There was a place in the city where the children on one side of the street wouldn't let the children on the other side come over. If a girl wanted to go to the store for her mother, she had to go out the back way and through the alley and all the way around the block. If the boys on one side of the street caught a dog that belonged to somebody on the other side, they would tie tin cans to its tail.

The children on one side would sit on their doorsteps all day long and point their fingers at the children on the other side. They would make noises like machine guns. " *A-a-a-a-a-a-a-a-a-a-a* " they would rattle until their throats were sore. That's all they did the whole day.

They couldn't even bounce balls or play marbles or jacks. They had to be on guard all the time because sometimes a mud ball or a stick or a stone would come flying across the street. The children on each side had to be ready to duck. There was nothing but trouble. No fun at all!

There was only one time when things were different. That was on very hot days when the firemen would come and open a fireplug on the street so that the children could play in the water.

" Open one for us and one for them," the children would ask.

The firemen would say, " Nothing doing! One for all and all for one! "

If the children wanted to go into the water, they had to go in together. But they didn't fight each other. When the strong streams of water came spurting out they were too busy fighting the water and catching their breath and laughing.

One hot day when they were playing in the water, little Schatzie, who lived on one side, fell down. Big Lillie, who lived on the other side, carried her screaming to her mother. " She fell in the deep part," said Lillie, still laughing from the fun and forgetting about sides.

After that Ethelyn began to wonder why they couldn't forget about sides all the time. Of course the firemen wouldn't turn the water hydrants on every day, but there must be *something* else the children could do together. Her throat hurt from making the machine-gun noises and her head hurt where a stone had hit it. " It's silly to go on like this," she decided, and she went out the back way and around the block to take a long walk by herself.

Ethelyn walked and walked until she came to a street she had never been on before. Down that street was coming something she had never seen before, either.

" What is it? " she asked a lady who was standing there looking too.

" It's a parade," said the lady.

Ethelyn stayed and watched the whole parade. First there were policemen on horses, walking slowly. Next were some men all dressed up in fancy hats. Then came a man walking alone, lifting his knees way up. He had a big gold stick that he moved up and down. The men walking behind him with horns played music as fast or as slow as he moved the stick. When he turned around and stopped walking, they stopped walking. When he put his stick down, they stopped blowing the horns. When he lifted his stick, they put their horns in their mouths. And when he moved his stick, they began to play the music again.

After the horns came some cars all decorated with colored paper that blew in the wind, then some more people dressed up. The parade was wonderful. Ethelyn stayed to the very end.

On the way home she had an idea. She kept on the lookout for a long piece of cardboard and a piece of wood that was burned black on one end. When she found them, she printed on the cardboard with the black end of the stick, " Giv up & well tel U sumpin." Then she took the sign home.

Ethelyn told the other children on her side of the street about the parade and how it would be almost as much fun for them all as playing in the water. She showed them the cardboard sign, and they held it up so the children on the other side could see it.

Soon a sign appeared on their side of the street. It said, " We wont giv up."

Ethelyn told her friends more about the parade. They let her print another sign. It said, " Kum over. Well tell U anyway."

They came over. Two boys began to wrestle right away, but Ethelyn and Lillie pulled them apart. Soon everybody was listening as Ethelyn told them about the parade.

" What I want to know is," she said at last, " why can't we have a parade down our street? "

" No horns! " yelled the kids.

" Who cares? " said Ethelyn. " The important thing is to tootle with your mouths or something when I move the stick — and stop when I put it down."

The children began to see that it was something like a game they played called " Follow the Leader."

" Only we have to get all dressed up for this," said Ethelyn. " Go home and find something to dress up in."

Everybody scattered. Ethelyn found an old wastebasket her mother said she could have. She put it on for a hat. She used a broom for a stick. Others came back with scarves and paper hats. One boy had a flag. Another boy had a cooking pot on his head!

" 'Tenshun! " said Ethelyn, lifting her stick. She moved it up and down, and the tootling and the parade began.

" This is much better than throwing things." she thought as she held her head as high as she could. " Nobody has to duck."

# Friendly Song

Florence Schulz　　　　　　　　　　　　　Old Folk Tune

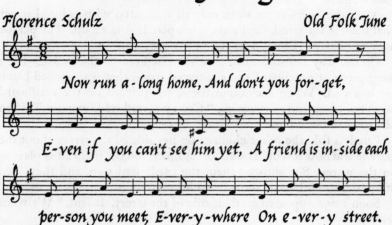

Now run a-long home, And don't you for-get,

E-ven if you can't see him yet, A friend is in-side each

per-son you meet, E-ver-y-where On e-ver-y street.

It's time to go home
And let's not forget
Things we've learned
And people we've met.
This very same thing
I say unto you:
You are my friend!
Am I your friend too?

There is a friend
In me and in you
Wherever we go,
Whatever we do.
Let's let him get out,
Let's let him go free,
The friend that's in you,
The friend that's in me.

We look all around
And what do we see?
Things are not
The way they could be.
So let's make a change
Here's what we can do:
You be my friend,
And I'll be yours too.

Now run along home
And look all around.
There may be
Some friends to be found.
This very same thing
I say unto you:
You be a friend,
You'll find a friend too.

This little camp song tune (" Now Run Along Home and Jump into Bed ") is catchy and easy to learn. You may want to make up your own words and use it as a good-by song or you may want to try one of the above verses.

# Grace

do  re  mi  fa  sol  la  ti

God, be-fore we eat and drink,
Of all the love and care you

do  ti  la  sol  fa  mi  re  do

We stand here qui-et-ly   to think
Send to us with every new-found friend.

# My Father's Children

### FRIENDSHIP SONG

Negro spiritual

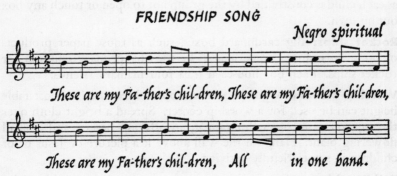

These are my Fa-ther's chil-dren, These are my Fa-ther's chil-dren,

These are my Fa-ther's chil-dren,  All    in one band.

**Friendship Circle:**  Children and teachers stand in a ring with arms crossed in front, grasping the hand of the friend on either side as they sing the friendship song just before going home.

# Cardboard Boxes

There is one thing of value to children that they can have in great abundance in the inner city, cardboard boxes. Most storekeepers are glad to give children as many boxes as they want, *if they appear to collect them at the very time the shelves are being restocked.* Otherwise the boxes are cut apart and flattened to save space, or burned.

Perhaps you could role-play the dilemma of a storekeeper who promised to save boxes for a child who did not appear to pick them up at the agreed-upon time. Boxes, boxes everywhere, and no room for customers! This could lead to a discussion about one of the qualities of a friend — being aware of the needs and problems of others.

In a vacation church school cardboard boxes are valuable for:

**Wastebaskets:** Pickup work is much easier if there is a wastebasket in each work center. The boxes can be painted and decorated with a magazine picture. Or they can be covered with scraps of gift wrappings or wallpaper.

**Project storehouses:** A neat row of shoe boxes (or larger boxes if necessary), one for each child with his name clearly crayoned on the front, serves many purposes. These can be personal lockers, keeping safe the toy gun or the pack of cards the child has brought from home and can't seem to keep inside his pocket (after a reasonable showing and telling time). The boxes can store half-finished projects between sessions. They can be a means of teaching respect for personal rights as each child is constrained by the group not to open or touch any box but his own.

**Rocket ships:** Big cardboard boxes, such as those paper products or home furnishings come in, can be used by primary children for rocket ships. Each box houses at least four primary friends.

**Worship centers:** A good-sized cardboard box that is almost table height can be used for a worship center. Spread a bright cloth over the top, place an open Bible on it, an offering basket, and a small flowering plant. Hang on the wall above it a picture of Jesus or of children in some friendly activity.

**Building blocks:** Boxes with covers can be taped shut and used for building blocks. Collect all sizes: pill boxes, candy boxes, soap boxes, oatmeal boxes, small cartons. Building blocks provide a good cafeteria activity for primary children — and some juniors.

**Floor protectors:** Cardboard boxes flattened out make better floor coverings than newspapers when messy work is being done. They do not crumple and tear so quickly.

**Paint trays and easels:** Select a box with a base about the size of a chair seat. With a small saw or serrated knife, cut the box off the base, leaving a two-inch standing-up edge all around. Place this tray on a chair seat to hold paint cans. (If your group is rowdy, fill the tray with sand around the cans to keep them stable.) Cut notches on each side of the tray edge. Set a large piece of cardboard in the notches and lean it against the chair back. Easel paper can be clipped to this cardboard. (Send for the Equipment and Supplies Catalog listed in the bibliography. It will tell you where to buy easel brushes, powdered easel paint, easel paper, and real easels if you can afford them.)

# Assistants and Committees

Cafeteria activities and other projects mean overwhelming work for the teacher unless she enlists the help of the children. Children are proud to have small cardboard badges describing their offices. They can wear them, keep them in their pockets, or attach them to their name boards.

**The Preparer of the Paint** comes early every day to measure out the powdered poster paint, mix it with water to the consistency of thick cream, and spread fresh newspapers on the floor where the painting goes on. He stays late each day to wash the long brushes, to roll up the paint-spotted newspapers and throw them out, and to store the leftover paint in a cool place where it will not be spilled by others who use the church in the afternoon or evening.

**The Custodian of the Clay** has more to do after the session than before. Some of the clay is used up in purposeful work; some is played with just for fun and emotional release. The latter is gathered up at the end of the session and worked into balls the size of a large apple. A thumb hole is made in each ball and a teaspoon of water is put into each hole to keep the clay moist overnight. The balls are carefully stored in a plastic bag or a covered crock. The table is sponged off and the drop cloth below is shaken out and put back in place.

If you do not have a table with an easily washed surface, tack an oilcloth or a plastic cover on it. A canvas drop cloth on the floor under the table and chairs catches clay crumbs that fall even when all the children obey the rule to keep the clay on the table. (An old blanket or bedspread may serve the purpose too.)

**Other offices** are Collecters of Cardboard Boxes, Preparers of Juice and Cookie Snacks, Planners of Worship, and Runners of Errands.

# Friendship Projects

**The friendship book** suggested in the Resource Section of the primary textbook does not *have* to be a book. It may be a scarf, roll-hemmed by girls just beginning to use a needle, and autographed in indelible ink by all the friends in the group.

It may be a three-piece vest (make a newspaper pattern first) cut from bright-colored cambric. The small shoulder and side seams can be " tailored " by the owners and the front pieces autographed by friends. Cutting with pinking shears avoids the necessity of hemming all around. Seams can be stapled if the boys do not care to sew.

Neckerchief squares of bright cotton may be autographed too and worn by boys and girls alike. The edges can be fringed by pulling threads. Younger children can autograph these in crayons. Crayon marks can be " set " on cotton by pressing them face down, with a warm iron.

If electric woodburning tools can be rented or borrowed from some boy scout troop, all the children may take home friendship planks — boards into which all the names have been burned.

Ten-cent-store white sailor caps may be given to the children for autographing.

**Friendship pennants** may be cut from felt and names glued on that are made from macaroni alphabet letters, as suggested on page 33 in the junior textbook.

**Friendship trees** may be drawn or painted on brown paper. The name of the church can be printed along the trunk and the children's names on the branches. A real tree branch may be stuck into a ball of clay to make it stand erect. The whole thing can be painted with easel paint in bright blue, green, or red. The children's names can be printed on key tags and hung on the branches.

# Tissue Flowers

Use pastel-colored facial tissues. Pull out a sheet of tissue and carefully tear it along the middle fold. Notice the tissue is made of two-ply paper. Peel these sheets apart so that you have four pieces. Lay them one on top of each other, alternating the torn edges and straight edges. Accordion-pleat them together, making the short pleats about one-half inch wide. Slip a bobby pin across the middle and fold the pleats up and away from the open end of the bobby pin. Hold the pin firmly in your fingers as the stem of the flower. Separate and twist the paper at the head of the bobby pin until a carnation-like blossom begins to form. The torn edges of the tissues look very much like flower petals.

Use scotch tape or strong thread to fasten the flowers to a thirty-inch circle of cotton tape to make a lei.

# Ideas in Concrete Form

The thinking and discussing that goes on, the songs, the stories, the Bible talk — all may be expressed and illustrated by the children as they make peep shows (page 99 in the junior textbook) or paper theaters (page 44 in the junior textbook) and build scenes such as the three-dimensional community scenes suggested in the Resource Section of the primary textbook. Murals can be crayoned, painted, or cut and pasted on long strips of brown wrapping paper. Two-sided posters, illustrating do's and don't's in stick-figure drawings (see Resource Section of the primary textbook) can be made from shirt boards.

Ideas may be expressed in the same clay that was used as an outlet for aggressive feelings. They may be painted into scenic or symbolic easel pictures. They may be illustrated in a dramatic skit worked out by two or three children with a teacher. They may be expressed in litanies, stories, or choral readings (see Resource Section of the primary textbook) developed by committees of interested children.

# Mosaic Work

After the children have heard the story, "The Girl," (page 91 of this book) they may be interested in going on a treasure hunt to see what they can find in the way of bright and beautiful bits of glass and metal in their neighborhood. These treasures can be laid out in patterns in a thin spreading of moist clay or plaster of paris in a box-top frame.

If your neighborhood is not rich in bright treasures, grains of rice and broken bits of macaroni can be tinted with food coloring until they look like translucent bits of jewels. These will stick to a spot of glue on a paper or cardboard to make blossoms on crayoned stems, a whole garden of flowers, or random swirls and lines. On purple or dark green paper they make a lovely collage.

But don't stop here! The children may find dried beans, split peas, long green noodles, bottle caps, bits of wood, string, ribbon, rope, wire, buttons, scraps of denim, net, fur, feathers, or leather. All of these prized things can be glued or pasted into marvelous pictures and designs. Plastic bags are best for collecting; you can see what you have. *Elmer's Glue-All* is best for sticking; it dries clear and sticks to wood, paper, or cloth.

Write to Arts and Crafts Distributors, Inc., for a 160-page informative catalog of creative materials and for their leaflet on mosaic work. (See page 118 for address.) If your neighborhood is short in bits of colored glass or other such treasures, you may want to purchase a dozen bags (about $3.90 per dozen) of the tiny, crystal-like, colored stones sold for making mosaics. If you have enough expense money, you may want to buy some vinyl tile which the children can use to cover coffee cans, cigar boxes, milk bottles, wooden bowls, wood, or cardboard to convert them into useful and decorative gifts.

# Nature Study in the Inner City

The miracle of life and growth is truly wonderful whether it is examined in persons, animals, or plants. It is a clear revelation of God, the Creator. In the world today we can readily see his power at work. In fact, our own God-given abilities are as miraculous and obstacle-overcoming as seeds, but like seeds they lie dormant in the dark unless they are recognized for what they are and given half a chance to grow and develop.

Take a walk to some place where something green has pushed its way sunward through a crack in the concrete. Whatever grows in the inner city is particularly marvelous.

Plant marigold seeds in eggshells filled with rich earth. Plant bean seeds in blotter-lined glasses filled with sand. The beans should be placed between the blotter and the glass so that the root development as well as the upward growth may be watched.

Collect bugs, beetles, flies — anything that is alive. Be realistic enough to accept even cockroaches and bedbugs; then explain the dangers of keeping them or of aiding their propagation in any way. Caterpillars, worms, moths, even butterflies can sometimes be found in the inner city. Ants are fascinating to observe. Feed them crumbs and leaves from celery if there are no tree leaves and grasses around.

You don't need to be a scientist or an expert to help children study bugs. All you have to do is be interested and wonder with them. *All About the Insect World* by Ferdinand C. Lane is a good book to have available.

Look from the wonder and miracle of the bugs' instincts to the greater wonder and miracle of human beings as God has created them, with power to control their instincts — to evaluate and choose what they will do.

# Sand and Glue Work

Common sand or manufactured glitter, glue or paste, brushes, shirt cardboards or tablet backs, construction paper, scissors, pencils, punches, string or tape, pictures — these are the materials needed for this activity.

The idea is to add sparkle to a name tag, a picture, or a book cover. The first project may be to decorate the letters on the junior pupil's book as suggested in the junior textbook, page 18. Paste or glue is brushed carefully over a specific area. While it is still wet, sand or glitter is sprinkled over it. The surplus glitter or sand can be shaken off when the adhesive has dried.

Name tags may be made of construction paper with the names printed with large block letters. The initial letters can be decorated.

A name tag and a church name tag may be worn sandwich-board fashion over the shoulders. Two shirt cardboards are required for each child. He prints his name as large as he can on one, the name of the church on the other. He decorates the letters with sand and glue and punches holes in the upper corners of each board. They are laced together with string or tape, put on over the child's head, and worn with his name across the chest, the church's name across the back.

Magazine pictures, pictures the children have drawn or painted, or pictures for the worship center may be mounted on colored paper or cardboard. A narrow border of glue can be brushed around the edge and sprinkled with sand to make a glittery frame.

Juniors may want to go deeper into this work. Fine white sand, cornmeal, or salt can be colored by mixing it with powdered tempera. A design can be sketched on brown paper. Thin glue is then brushed over the area to be covered with the first color. The colored material is sprinkled on, the surplus shaken off, and then glue applied to the area to be covered with the second color, and so on. The finished picture can be " fixed " by spraying it with clear lacquer.

# Space-Travel Ideas

Moon rockets, rocket ships, and jet planes can be made tinkertoy fashion with toothpicks and soaked, dried peas. Buy dried peas — the whole kind, not split peas — and soak them about ten hours until they are bright green and completely softened. Have book and magazine pictures of planes and rocket ships around for the children to consult.

Primary children who do not know each other get to be friends quickly if they are divided into groups of four for snack time. Each group builds its own rocket ship of chairs, placed upside down or sideways, and sits inside. The teacher zooms from rocket to rocket on her own two feet, serving snacks to the various groups of friends.

If junior groups are astronaut- and rocket-minded, the relation of the earth to the other planets might be studied and worked out in papier-mâché balls. (Papier-mâché is made by soaking strips of newspaper in hot water for twenty-four hours until it is a pulpy mass, then adding either flour paste or laundry starch until modeling consistency is obtained.)

All sorts of rocket ships can be made of cardboard boxes.

# Table-top Panoramas

After inner-city children have taken a trip to the beach, to a forest preserve, or to a park, they may want to re-live their adventure by making a table-top panorama.

A miniature beach can be made of sand and water in a large tin tray. Pipe cleaners can be twisted together to make figures of children playing in the sun.

Clay can make the hills and dales of a forest preserve with twigs stuck in for trees. When the clay dries, it can be painted brown or green. Clumps of leaves on the trees or bushes can be represented by bits of sponges painted green. Tree trunks can also be modeled of clay, toothpicks can be the branches, and soaked, dried peas the leaves. Of course the children may have other ideas about details.

Having seen some greenery, the boys and girls may want to make a dish garden, Japanese style, or a terrarium or plant a window box for the church. Grass seed sowed in foil pans filled with earth produces almost instant greenery.

Juniors may want to make a panorama illustrating one of the Bible stories in the junior textbook, such as the ones on page 20 or 36.

# Water Play

Water on children's hands seems to subdue and quiet their excitements. Sudsy, foamy, bubbly water does the job even better.

Some of the big galvanized tubs for washing clothes are still available. An excited six- or seven-year-old might quiet down if he could spend a few minutes fashioning boats from pieces of wood, paper, or foil pans, and sail these about in a tub of water.

A dishpan with water may be placed in the housekeeping corner for washing dishes, dolls, or doll clothes.

Primary-age children enjoy water play activities as much as do younger children, and the water may serve a therapeutic need or stimulate dramatic activity. For instance, a table with a pan of water, a variety of plastic bottles of various shapes and colors, a few funnels and some spoons might become a drug store, a soda fountain or a chemist's laboratory. Older children might be trusted with small glass bottles and food coloring to add interest to this play. At times this play may be related to the purposes of the session as when the group is led to think of the ways the druggists in their neighborhoods — whatever their national or racial origin — contribute to the life of the community.

# When You Are at Your Wit's End

Working with inner-city children is admittedly very difficult and trying at times. When foolishness, teasing, or downright battles interrupt the busy hum of purposeful activity in your group, there are certain points for you to consider in dealing with the situation.

**1.** The children (or one particular child) may simply need to let off steam because they (or he) have been concentrating too long at one task. A lively game for the group or an errand for the individual child may remedy the trouble.

**2.** Some foolishness, some horsing around, must be overlooked as what Dr. Fritz Redl aptly calls a "waste by-product of normal development."

**3.** A sort of mob hysteria breaks out sometimes and carries even the best-behaved children along with it. Beware of trying to find the child who started it. This will give him great status in the eyes of his fellows. Any group is collectively responsible for its behavior and should be held to this responsibility.

**4.** Finally, there is some misbehavior that is due to neurotic fears and anxieties that are too deeply embedded to be uncovered and treated except professionally. Your ministry, however devoted, may not be able to reach every child. You may have to find an adult to stand by ready to whisk away the constant offender at the first sign of annoying behavior each day. Keep him away from the group, work with him individually, and meanwhile try to find some counseling service for him and his family. Don't be too quick to put a child in this category, but don't try your own patience too long either. There are limits to what one teacher can do in any situation.

# BOOKS FOR CHILDREN

*All About the Insect World* by Ferdinand C. Lane. Random House, New York, 1954.

*The Skyscraper* by Yen Liang. J. B. Lippincott Company, Philadelphia, 1958. (A story of old streets with crowded shabby buildings where children had no place to play and people hardly ever saw the sun. People worked together to do something about the situation. Machines, skillful hands, trucks, sewer pipes are all pictured dramatically. Then the beautiful new skyscraper is shown.)

*The World in a City Block* by Natalie Hall. Viking Press, New York, 1960. (This is the story of the son of a big-city baker who was sad because his older brother had gone off to join the merchant marines. He wished he could see the world too. As he goes around his neighborhood, taking over his brother's job of delivering bread, he discovers fascinating people and places that he never before realized could be found so close to home.)

# CATALOGS AND PAMPHLETS

Age Group Charts: *the primary child, the lower junior child, the junior child.* The Board of Christian Education and Publication of the Evangelical and Reformed Church and the Division of Christian Education of the Board of Home Missions of the Congregational Christian Churches, 1957. Order from the Division of Christian Education of the Board for Homeland Ministries of the United Church of Christ, 1505 Race Street, Philadelphia 2, Pennsylvania.

*All in Play* by Rowena M. Shoemaker. Play Schools Association, Inc., 41 West 57th St., New York 19, New York. (Part III tells about materials that can be obtained without much money.)

*Catalog of Equipment and Supplies*, Association for Childhood Education International, 1200 15th Street, N.W., Washington 5, D. C.

*Children can make it!* Association for Childhood Education, Washington, D. C. (Tells how to make things that work from milk containers, soda straws, paper clips, spools and wires, newspapers, paper bags, coat hangers and the like.)

*Handbook for Recreation.* U. S. Department of Health, Education and Welfare. Superintendent of Documents, U. S. Government Printing Office, Washington 25, D. C.

*Mosaics.* Arts & Crafts Distributors, Inc., 9520 Baltimore Avenue, College Park, Maryland.

*You Can Do It!* by Altha S. Bowman, Ralph Berry, Margaret M. Clemens. The Judson Press, Philadelphia, 1943.

# HYMNALS AND SONGBOOKS

*Hymns for Junior Worship.* The Westminster Press, Philadelphia, 1940.

*Hymns for Primary Worship.* The Westminster Press, Philadelphia, 1946.

*Little Songs on Big Subjects* (paperback). Argosy Music Corporation, 631 Orienta Ave., Mamaroneck, N. Y. Also available from the CMC Division of Columbia University Press, 1125 Amsterdam Avenue, New York 25, New York.

*Sing, Children, Sing* by Edith Lovell Thomas. Abingdon-Cokesbury Press, Nashville, 1939.

*The Whole World Singing* by Edith Lovell Thomas. Friendship Press, New York, 1950.